The Economics and Strategies of Data Security

The Economics and Strategies of Data Security

Daniel E. Geer, Jr., Sc.D.
Verdasys

Table of Contents

The Economics and Strategies of Data Security

Foreword

I'm delighted and honored to introduce this book, the first in a series of three volumes for business leaders, security practitioners and operations managers. This volume explores the dramatic shift from infrastructure protection to information protection explaining why data security is critical to business today. The book describes how implementing successful data security solutions across sophisticated global organizations requires a new data-centric, risk based strategic approach.

The founding of our company, Verdasys was based on an actual data security breach, not defined in an engineering lab but in a real company (my previous firm) where hundreds of millions of dollars worth of intellectual property was nearly stolen with potentially catastrophic results. The data theft incident led the founders of Verdasys to discover that a major problem existed and there was no reasonable, serious, cost-effective solution available.

In defining the requirements of our data security solution, Digital Guardian, we initially focused on the incident that we had experienced, and saw quickly how many other companies were in the same predicament; worried about the same problems without effective solutions available. In fact, the problems of data security had been largely ignored by major vendors. In the process of developing our technology and interacting with prospective customers we uncovered broad, high-value and significant unsolved problems. We all wrestled with the same questions: "How do I manage the risk of losing or compromising sensitive data while sharing as much information as possible to enable my business to be more agile and competitive?" "How do I implement cost-effective, flexible control over my data in a way that transcends the traditional infrastructural boundaries of IT security — in short, how do I do data-centric security?"

As we ventured forth we were amazed at how many others were beginning to see the need for data security solutions to a broad array of complex use cases and challenges. With our customers we've witnessed a real shift from infrastructure or network security to data security. A number of significant, permanent and growing trends driving this shift have emerged clearly over the past few years. These include increased data mobility, growing data value, a rising tide of privacy and compliance legislation targeted at data as well as ever more sophisticated professionalized hackers. In addition there is an ongoing fundamental shift in the way large global organizations distribute or outsource knowledge based business processes. All these challenging trends contribute to a real need for a new way to think about and implement data security solutions.

The dramatic increase in data breaches alone has driven the world's best companies to adopt a new proactive approach to data security beyond the traditional network or infrastructure standards of the past. Traditional infrastructural and network based approaches are necessary but insufficient to fulfill the broad set of data security business problems of global organizations moving forward.

It is into this breach, no pun intended, that Verdasys has leapt. This is where our series of books, thinking and strategies all converge — the shift from infrastructure protection to information protection. The dislocation of requirements from operational integrity to business process integrity drives a shift from the various network and infrastructure layers to a data-centric focused approach and data security. This does not mean a bunch of infrastructure products glued together and plugged into a "unified" console. It means a well thought out differentiated strategy, technology framework and solution driven approach for real-time information risk management.

Verdasys also heralds the beginning of the end of the Sisyphean practice of securing corporations in wave after wave of reactive point product implementations. The old approaches are not only economically damaging but if you simply look at the headlines on any given day — they're not working. Our goal is to define strategies that will deliver a smooth continuum of solutions to an interrelated set of high-value data security challenges today and well into the future.

Verdasys developed our technology foundation on two simple notions — tell me what happened to my data and how I can control it without impacting productivity? The first task was to enable, for the first time ever, a transactional level understanding of data usage independent of content, device, network or application. The second goal was to implement infrastructure and application independent data controls without a loss or impact to productivity.

Digital Guardian has been expanded, with phenomenal input from our customers representing a cross section of the world's largest and most respected companies, into an enterprise solution that enables companies to economically, intelligently and adaptively address the broadest set of expanding information risk use cases. I'm very happy to report that to date Verdasys technologies have interdicted the potential loss of well over six hundred million dollars worth of data in disclosed incidents. Perhaps unique amongst any data security vendor we have provided proof, via our technology, resulting in the levying of a fine of one hundred million dollars on an organization found guilty of data theft (the largest single fine of its kind to date).

This first book, The Economics and Strategies of Data Security, defines the concepts and economics of a sound data security strategy and assists managers in understanding the full extent of risks and costs associated with data loss. The ideas expressed in this volume are ones we've discussed and refined in conversations with hundreds of CISOs, CIOs, CEOs and business leaders. The goals of the book are to encourage discussion around the economics of data security, define intelligent data-centric strategies and perhaps most boldly, develop at the technical level a forward looking approach that will address data security needs both today and tomorrow.

I hope that you enjoy this book as much as I have enjoyed developing and seeing these ideas in action with customers, partners, advisers and our team. My sincere wish is that you find it useful for anything from sparking meaningful dialogue within your organizations all the way to defining and building your own data security strategy and choosing solutions. Thank you for picking up a copy and we hope to see you in our exciting and ever challenging field of endeavor.

Sincerely Yours,

Seth Birnbaum, CEO
Verdasys, Inc.

The Economics and Strategies of Data Security

Acknowledgements

The books of men do not appear out of thin air, and as this book is about economics one must be mindful that the cost of anything is its foregone alternative. The author therefore thanks the decision makers at Verdasys for choosing to forego other deliverables thus to provide the necessary free space and time to write this book — free to me but not to them, of course. They are: Allen Michels, Chairman, Seth Birnbaum, CEO, and Nick Stamos, President.

The author has been lucky as well to have had the chance to make so many errors over time and yet to live to tell about it. Don't ever discount how much more efficient it is to learn from practice and theory together than from either alone. To the many who have reinforced Nietzche's dictum — "That which does not kill me makes me stronger." — thank you, whether you like it or not.

In theory, there is no difference between theory and practice, but, in practice, there is.

1. Introduction

This is a book about data security, both about data and about security as well as about the union of the two. It is written for those who are responsible for both, willingly or otherwise, technically oriented or not, driven by governance concern or a sense of risk and duty. It is not written for early adopters nor is it written for laggards. By assumption, you, the reader, do not have a need for anyone to tell you which button to press, but you do need to know how to think about data security so that you can make decisions that work — more importantly, decisions that last. You need to make data security a core part of your strategy but, as always, at the lowest reasonable cost both in monetary costs and, which is more, in the costs of organizational complexity. You need to know how to lead the target.

You can see that this book is small. It is small to make it useful; brevity may be the soul of wit but wit is the soul of brevity, too. While not entirely perfect, the chapters are arranged in a way that makes it possible to read and re-read them separately and, perhaps, to make it plausible for you to have specific chapters pushed out to your co-workers and subordinates. For this they must and do overlap slightly. Each chapter has that same structured form as a good speech — a few bullets to tell you what the chapter is going to say, a prose body that says it, and a summary of what the chapter said. The present author can think of no higher compliment than were you, the reader, to steal everything from single sentences to great swathes of this book for your own purposes. Steal away.

In the same spirit as each chapter, this is what the book as a whole is going to say. As an introduction, we talk about why we are here, which simply is that data is where the money is, data is where the risk is, and data is where the future is. To do that we have to characterize what data is and how what it is will change during your career lifetime. This comes down to an attempt to characterize data's volume, data's mobility, and data's value which you can think of as much like a physicist would talk about mass, momentum, and charge, or a banker would think of capital, leverage, and volatility.

We'll next take a side excursion into how we got to where we are. Old timers can skip this, but since security was hardly ever at the top of anyone's list of things to do until after their system had enough users to be dangerous, perhaps we can learn from this history what next to expect. This is especially important as the underlying timescale of how hardware develops itself drives what is the economically optimal computer. To summarize that in a sentence, computing and networking alike are now about staggering amounts of data, all of it in motion.

Taking that as a given, much the same way an avalanche on the hill above you quickly becomes a given, we will look at how data security is more business than technical concern. This has lots of ways to look at it, from liability to revenue protection to conservation of intangible assets to counterparty risk as a business issue to law enforcement and the rules of evidence to data's place in disaster recovery regimes. As with most business matters, good enough will be good enough and, therefore, the problem is how to determine what is good enough — not that any of this stands still, mind you.

Choice. The problem is choice. Solutions themselves begin and end with choice. We will explore a variety of choices such as the incremental reform strategy *vs.* the big-bang strategy, the apparent regulatory need to prove a negative *vs.* the security need just to recognize that which is negative, the choices that differentiate treating data security as a tax *vs.* as an investment, and even whether the asymmetric war we are in is worth winning *vs.* whether just diverting attacks to others is good enough, all against the axiomatic backdrop that data security is a means, not an end, and that there is and always will be a conflict between the best & the good. The high point of this will be just how much security thought is today a generalized risk management approach yet how much of it is not, because of the way that security for data differs from security for candy bars, train cars, or movie stars.

If we limit our choices to just what we choose to do next, the problem remains hard, and the economics the solution space pretty much have to rule. We will discuss the kind of strategies that favor specificity with one-to-one solutions, *i.e.*, solutions with are clearly the best at what they do and which kill some kind of pathogen dead. We will discuss the kind of strategies that favor versatility instead, *i.e.*, where there is some chance of a one-to-many mapping — one solution to many problems, but never perfect. In all of this, we will be remembering that on the cost side of the ledger what we are really doing is a classic economic balancing game: balancing protection costs and clean-up costs for the most economically favorable impact on the firm. To illustrate this as best we can, here and there we provide worked models, suitable for stealing.

Because we are writing this when we are, it is both needful and timely to talk about how data security interplays with security metrics. This includes, fundamentally, what it is that can be measured, if, for no other reason, we do not want to try to measure something that will only waste our time or fool us. We will compare and contrast measurement as score keeping, measurement as predictive tool, and measurement for decision support, possibilities that do not contradict each other so long as we keep sight of what we are doing. We will be specific to what is unique about data and its measurement.

If we are to speak the language that our intended readers speak, we have to speak the language of the market. This includes the nature of the market including the data security market, especially as any new market is uniquely vulnerable to charlatans and hype. We will have some observations on why technical and business justifications never match, and why market analysts cannot afford to pick winners on rational grounds. We will explore, but perhaps discouragingly, how complexity is the enemy of security when nearly every so-called security solution risks adding complexity to the enterprise. We will remind ourselves that perhaps the highest goal for any security product is how to be future-proof in a world where the evolution of threat is dizzyingly fast and the data security solutions that matter are the ones whose effective value is not limited to a brief moment in the sun while some particularly new attack is running rampant. Similarly, we will remind ourselves that the most stringent constraint on any security product is that it not be a threat in and of itself, which is harder than it sounds and which requires that all security products be met with skepticism. We will give some advice on how to challenge a vendor on all these points.

There is, of course, a wrapup at the end. If you are of the mind that "Life is short, eat dessert first," then go there now, but like the classic advice to a speechmaker, the wrap will tell you what we have already told you, though perhaps in a more succinct way.

And let us, just here at the outset, remind you as if you didn't already know that time is your enemy. Perhaps you think that about everything, but for the purposes of this book, time is your enemy in all matters around data security. A science fiction writer might be better on this topic than a scientist writer, but we are certainly agreed that human reaction times are no longer an effective time constant for data security protections. If you need to have some statistics and some trend numbers to explain this sort of point to others, particularly any point about how purely reactive mechanisms are unlikely to provide effective security, perhaps you will find something of value here.

It is, of course, no surprise that we are putting into action many of the ideas in this book. One can call that crass commercialism, putting your money where your mouth is, or just saying what you mean and meaning what you say. While neither we nor you are perfect, part of getting value out of protecting value is to not avoid letting the best to be the enemy of the good. This sense of tradeoff is central to security thought and to effective products. My colleagues and I offer the Verdasys Digital Guardian as an example of an astutely abstracted, appropriately humble, future proof mechanism for data management including but not limited to security. The core idea of Digital Guardian is that there will never be an end to new kinds of misuse, and that the misuse that is the hardest to see will become the misuse that most endangers the firm. We want to believe that the more informed you are, the more you will agree with us, which is, in fact, why we are here.

So, let's get to it, shall we?

Dan Geer
November, 2007

We can tell when a technology has truly arrived when the new problems it gives rise to approach in magnitude the problems it was designed to solve.

— *Arthur Chandler, 1997*

2. How we got here / Punctuated equilibria in computing's timeline

There's never been an industry before that moved as fast as this one, but you know that and you are tired of reading it. We would like, however, to trace data and thus data security through the timeline. It will be quick, so speed read if you like.

Just realize this: The entire security industry as we know it here traces to when the invention of the browser forced Microsoft to put a TCP/IP stack in Windows 95. That is ancient news now, but Stephen Jay Gould's great contribution to paleontology was to show that evolution is never a smooth ramp, but rather long straightaways between hairpin turns.[1] The Internet, the browser, and our security industry all were part of the last hairpin turn. Today, and because of data security, we're skidding into another one, but let's start at the beginning.

2.1. Standalone - you take what you can get

At the outset, a computer was too expensive to play with, connected to nothing but itself, and was taken rather seriously. Data, such as it was, meant a few numbers — mostly counts of physical things. Data did not live in the computer except when it was running and attended, and questions of data access, data retention,

[1] Eldredge N & Gould SJ, "Punctuated equilibria: an alternative to phyletic gradualism," in Schopf TJM, ed., Models in Paleobiology, 1972, Freeman Cooper, pp82-115.

and data integrity didn't even come up beyond controlling who got to be in the room with the computer. Figure 1 approximates this, with the user and the data as a unit (that at least arrived and left together).

That sort of computer is uninteresting in our present context, but it's nevertheless worth remembering that data was not "always on." Quite the contrary, nothing could get at the data. The computer was a serially re-usable appliance, something where this and that did not interfere with each because it was impossible for them to do so. This single-purposeness coupled with disconnectedness is worth remembering as data security was irrelevant outside of government classification systems. If we can call it that, then, hairpin turn #1 was the creation of an electronic data processing unit itself and, with it the creation of the concept of data as

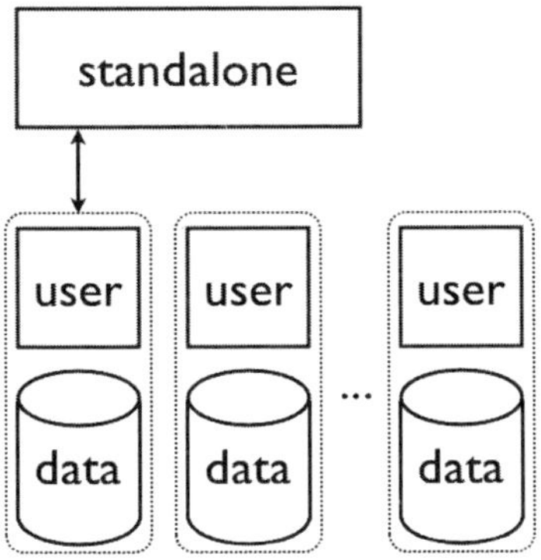

Figure 1: The standalone computer, to which you brought data

something which was a kind of fodder and repository of value. Nevertheless, stealing data while your program had the computer to itself was about as plausible as stealing your pants while you had them on.

2.2. Time-share - move data to where computing is

Time-share's development had a classic economic motivation, to make the computing more affordable and thus more available, especially to more people but also to a broader class of problems. We all know how it worked: When not busy with one task the computer would be working on another. If busy all the time, then everyone just had to take turns. The cost effectiveness rose because the duty cycle rose, and user communities could effectively pool funds for their mutual benefit. Universities led the way in most cases. Figure 2 approximates this next stage, with the user and the data as a unit for execution but the users came and went and the data stayed with the timeshare system.

Now when there was a time-share machine, and you were entitled to a slice, then you went to where it was, *i.e.*, you took your data to where the computing was. You did this in a variety of ways, but overall the density of the media on which data was stored rose fast enough that, soon enough, your data lived where the computing was and you didn't actually take it there because it already was there. This was a shift, and a rather remarkable one, but the data security implications were almost entirely these two: (1) availability — you data had better be where you left it, and (2),

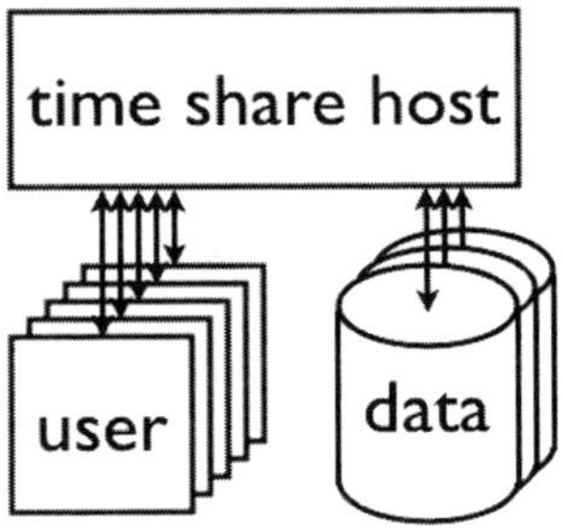

Figure 2: The timeshare computer, which you shared and with which you left your data

segregated user space — your run-time slice of the computer was protected from everyone else's run-time slice (if only to avoid collisions). If nothing else, timeshare was the nativity of the backup tape, and a transfer of responsibility for data protection from the owner of it to an agent of that owner, at least insofar as data availability was concerned. Again, no computer was so cheap as to be unattended or taken anything but seriously, and if you misbehaved enough to get yourself banned you would no longer have computer access at all. There is, after all, nothing like scarcity and a gatekeeper to it for creating the wherewithal for discipline. Timeshare did make computing independent of time constraints; you no longer had to queue or make an appointment. So: Hairpin turn #2 was that your data not only existed and was valuable, but that others cared for it as it lived where it belonged which was not where you lived.

2.3. Distributed client-server - move computing to where data is

The IBM Personal Computer (PC) appeared in August, 1981, followed in May, 1982, by SUN's first workstation and in January, 1984, by Apple's first Macintosh. In between those events, on January 1, 1983, the ARPAnet converted to all TCP/IP, and the Internet began. The client server model followed, led by finance, largely in New York City, and in a small number of universities.[2] That does not do the hairpin turn this represented justice, but that is what it was — a coincidental appearance of cheap computing and the potential for universal inter-connectivity, what SUN famously described as "The network is the computer." Figure 3 approximates client-server, *per se*, with the user and the data back to being a unit for execution but execution being at the user's end of the wire, augmented by services that included data transfer up and down from servers for retention.

The client server model, coupled to Moore's Law (of a continuous eighteen-month doubling of performance-to-price for computer processing), quickly changed the dynamic around "data processing" from one where the data is brought to where the computing is to one where computing is brought to where the data

[2] The present author was associated with one of these, Project Athena at MIT, but there were several others including North Carolina State, Iowa, Michigan, Brown, Carnegie Mellon, Maryland College Park, *etc.*

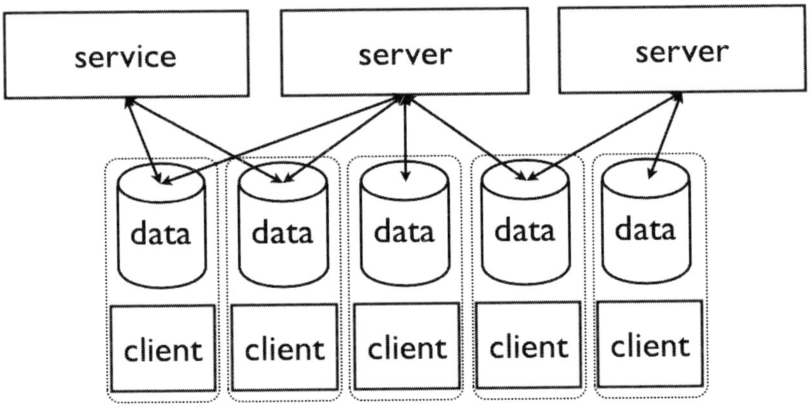

Figure 3: The client-server model, where data was provided to you

is. In retrospect, this seems obvious and perhaps even banal, but at the time it was not banal at all as, *inter alia*, this allowed data to be much fresher and to change faster since it did not have to be packaged and hand carried to where the user stood in some queue. This is why finance, in particular, picked up the model. Distributed computing changed finance from a who-you-know game to a kind of technologic warfare with desktop computing supported by servers. The computer was where the data and decision maker were, supported by servers of various sorts but primarily as sources of data.

Computing was no longer scarce, but suddenly the outcome was only as good as the data, and the data was frequently only as good as the algorithms that massaged it. The security implications of this came soon enough as that which the server offered probably ought only to go to those who deserved. By 1985, the idea of network-based authentication was already in place and by 1988 today's most deployed system for that, Kerberos,[3] was in widespread use. In this model, data lived where the computing now was, but it sometimes was moved there from server-based repositories. Network-centric authentication formed the basis for permissions to do those movements, but there was little else and no threat profile beyond preventing the inappropriate person from getting data in the first place. So, hairpin turn #3 added location-independence to the timeshare world's time-independence, and thus began the need for authentication and availability protections. From a data security point of view, that change caused companies everywhere to implement access control systems.

---

[3] Steiner J, Neuman BC, & Schiller J, "Kerberos: An Authentication Service for Open Network Systems," Proceedings, USENIX Technical Conference, Dallas, Texas, Winter 1988.

As an aside, the so-called "Orange Book" was published[4] in 1983. The ordinary course of a security publication such as the Orange Book would have become a normative influence on the computing industry at large. However, the disruptive arrival of personal computing as historically cheap as the IBM PC, the SUN workstation, and the Apple Macintosh caused the Orange Book to have nearly no commercial influence at all because when everyone wants their own computer the Department of Defense's buying power no longer steers the computing industry. We'll come back to the Orange Book shortly.

2.4. SOA is the return of time-share - but data is everywhere

The "Service Oriented Architecture" (SOA) idea is just that, an idea; it is not a hard standard. It can be said to extend the client-server model by a relaxation of interface: from defined protocols between known entities to self-describing protocols where the entities have no direct calls to each other. As such, the entities are one to three orders of magnitude larger (times 10-1000) than with the sort of tight coupling that modular programming, say, would anticipate. Figure 4 has a picture of SOA, with the increasing complexity made

[4] Trusted Computer System Evaluation Criteria (TCSEC), National Computer Security Center (NCSC), 1983.

intentionally obvious. but the core idea is simple: Services, however and by whomever they are constructed, are the building blocks rather than programmers' conventional modules.

As such, there is a wealth of metadata, typically in something like the "extensible markup language" (XML), that describes both the services and the data that those services handle. The hope in all this is that the Nth implementation using these components is essentially free. This is, as you know, the same hope expressed by every preceding technology for reuse of software, only much bigger.

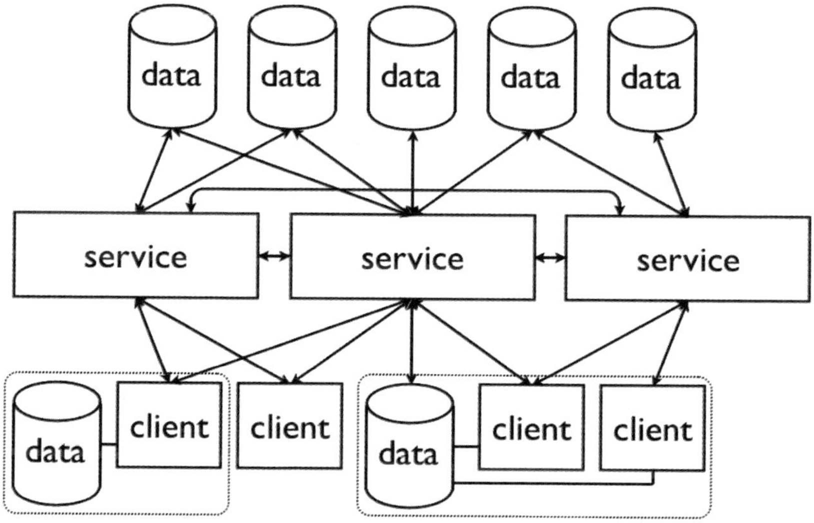

Figure 4: SOA, which is like timeshare but the data is everywhere

The relevance to data security is this: SOA is timeshare revisited, but with the data in no particular place. Timeshare was "move the data to where the computing is" with the quaint side condition that "where the computing is" actually had some meaningful definition. With SOA there is no quaintness; there is no "there" there and that is, ignoring data security, a decided economic advantage, time-independence and location-independence become, with SOA, time- and location-irrelevant, perhaps even undiscoverable. With data security in mind, the absence of any defined fixed point in either space or time is an enormous challenge and one which relies on services to do what used to be the data's owner's responsibility — to know where data is and who has access. Add to this the general statelessness of "web services" and it is clear that the data is as hard to protect as water is to sweep. Where this goes is not as yet certain, but it almost surely implies that data must either become self-protecting (massive amounts of encryption and the conversion of passive data objects into miniature program fragments), or the endpoints where services and users come together will have be very well instrumented indeed. We find the latter more plausible.

The going-forward challenge of data protection under SOA is akin to challenges that had heretofore been the province of the intelligence community. There, many bits of information that may each be easy to obtain or effectively meaningless by themselves produce a sum that is very much greater than the parts, and that sum is what is protected with such vigor. In the commercial world, the same is true. As an experiment, you can probably get twenty people in a large room to each answer one embarrassing question, but no one person will willingly answer twenty embarrassing questions in that same large room, illustrating that nearly everyone intuitively knows that data fusion is powerful. With respect to data security, that might also be said to be our challenge — to protect the whole by protecting the parts. Factually, however, we can no longer locate the whole in whole, only the parts remain locatable and barely that. The sum — that which is greater than the parts — comes together evanescently and on demand, and therefore it is at the point of use that any protections have to be done. There is no other place, there is no other time, there is no other facility than to surveil the assemblage and use of data than where it all comes together. We should have perhaps wished for this insight before we made data protection so enormously difficult, but facing facts, pictures like Figure 4 are not going to get simplified except by force and, therefore, the challenge is to find a way to manipulate a pressure point upstream of where the bleeding is, not to try to undo the wound.

2.5. The profound impact of differential change at the hardware level

It must be remembered that computing does not change just because programmers get more clever. Far from it — the hardware folks are winning and have been winning for a long time. Everyone has heard of Moore's Law and the doubling of how much data processing you can get for a dollar every eighteen months. Historically speaking, that kind of change in an industrial value equation is unprecedented and yet it continues. But a computer is made of three things — the CPU, the data storage principally on disk, and the transmission speed across available networks. Data storage doubles faster than CPU capacity does and for the purposes of rough numbers and inference, it is fair to say that the doubling time is circa twelve months. Bandwidth in the laboratory doubles faster still and, again, for the purposes of rough numbers and inference, we'll call that doubling time nine months. In pictures, Figure 5 shows this as a graph where the punchline is that, when carried over a decade, computing horsepower rises by two orders of magnitude but data rises by three and bandwidth by four. In other words, if we kept building the kinds of computers we have today, CPU horsepower per unit of data would fall by 90% even while the amount of data that could be moved per unit time would rise by a factor of ten.

These laboratory results are neither precise nor entirely smooth, but after years of predictability it would be folly to bet against them even if they are approximations. Put differently, rate constants like these mean it will not be software change that drives the data protection agenda going forward, at least not in the sense of the causal factors for why data gets to be ever more the issue, but rather hardware. This will be

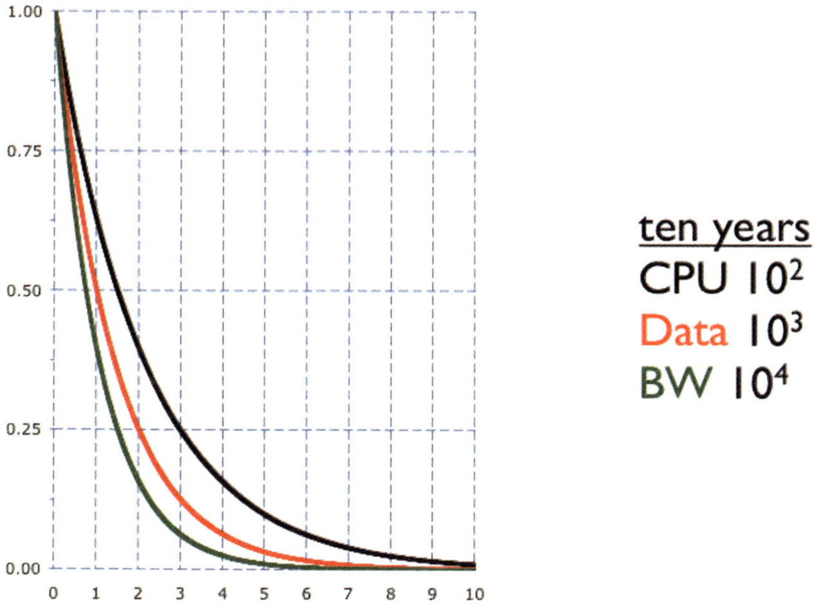

Figure 5: Lab-driven optimality

especially true as embedded devices assume total dominance because, if nothing else, embedded devices will be little observed and their contribution to the data flood will largely be unstructured.

In parallel, the general purpose computer is, for all practical purposes, dead as a desirable commodity product; every corporate enterprise and most home users effectively want appliances, not general purpose machines. General purpose machines are ones that enable total reconfiguration, something the corporate world wants only at rare moments but a few competent

> *Dateline today:*
> Automobiles already have more embedded systems than they do passengers, no one's programmers are getting twice as smart every eighteen months hence the ratio of skill to power is falling fast, and it is certainly cheaper to retain all data than to do careful selective deletion from it.

people want all the time. The difficulties of combating complexity's side effects become paramount the more complexity and power we have, and, as discussed just above, that power curve shows no signs of abating. This inevitably pushes computing down into smaller devices distributed more invisibly, yet this very ubiquity makes the data security problem harder. Stopping progress not being an option, we need a new model, one that aspires to be future-proof, and one which is instrumented enough that we can tell how well it is doing even if we cannot do as well at protecting ourselves as it does at protecting us — and we can't. We'll pause now for a side discussion.

To show the punctured equilibrium where the digital security industry was created, look at these three graphs. Figure 6 shows the rising number of reported information security incidents per year as reported to the Computer Emergency Response Team through 2003 (when CERT ceased publication of this number).

Starting with that, Figure 7 shows the rate of change in those numbers year over year, but with the timeline now

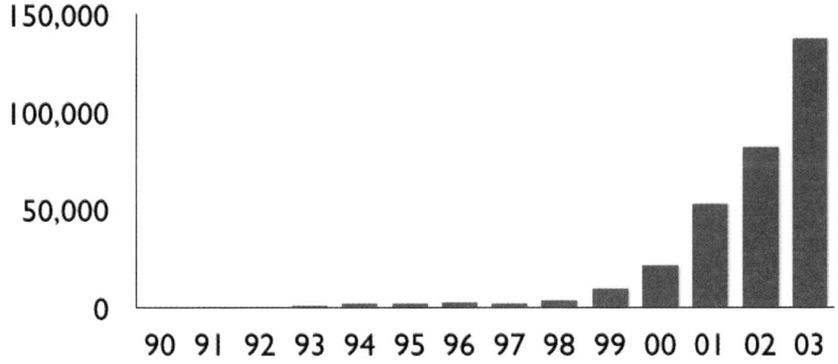

Figure 6: Incidents reported to the CERT

annotated with the (per IDC) dates of effective introduction of new models of the Microsoft operating system. (As the

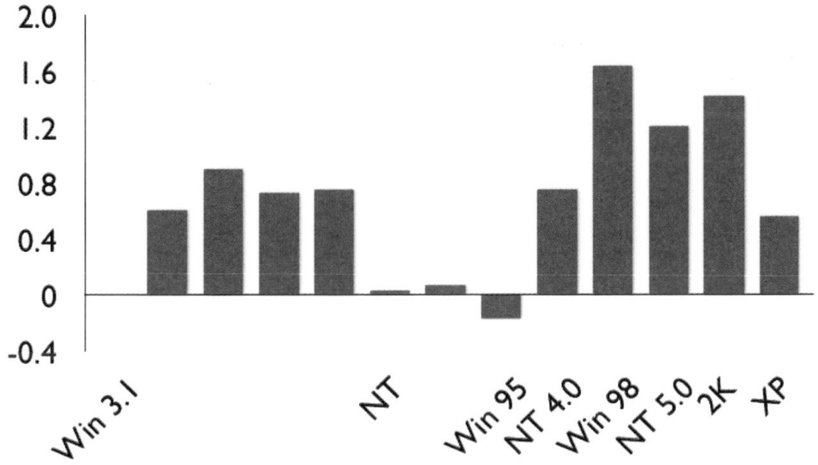

Figure 7: Rate of change against previous year, in percent

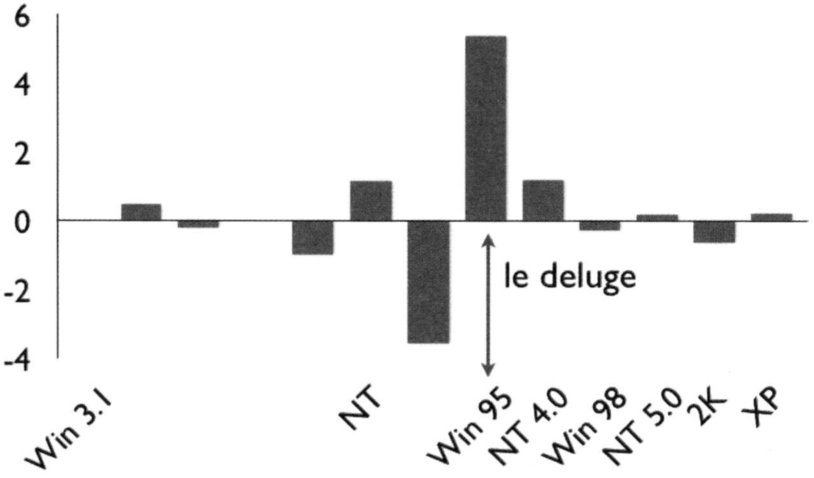

Figure 8: Change in rate of change year to year, as a ratio

Microsoft operating system is circa 95% of all desktops, one can speak of the Internet and Microsoft interchangeably.) In turn, Figure 8 shows the rate of change of the rate of change.

Yes, these are crude approximations of a first and a second derivative, but the point is in the last figure (8) and marked "le deluge." That point in time is one year after when Windows 95, the first Microsoft operating system with a built-in TCP/IP stack, appeared and coincident with the availability of a browser for it. That was what punctuated the (security) equilibrium then in place, such as it was, in that it took an operating system designed for a single owner-operator on, at most, a private low-speed network and attached it to the world. The digital security industry followed and, in particular, network and host security became where everyone had to be.

This is no indictment of Microsoft but rather an easy-to-show explanation of how "punctuated equilibria" exist in the inorganic world of networked computers as they do in biology.

It is the claim of this book that we are in a second moment of rapid evolutionary change. As we are in it, definitive, pretty pictures are not as easy to get, but our claim is this: Data security now replaces network and host security as the focus of the security professionals and the rules change. The equilibrium, such as it was, between offense and defense, between attack and defend, is fundamentally altered now that the attack class has largely rolled over from adventurers and braggarts to professionals.

First, the professionalization of the attack side is real. As perhaps the simplest indicium, one that you can share with colleagues, it appears that the attack side has a work week. Figure 9, shows the variation in the number of phishing e-mails received when plotted by day of the week.[5]

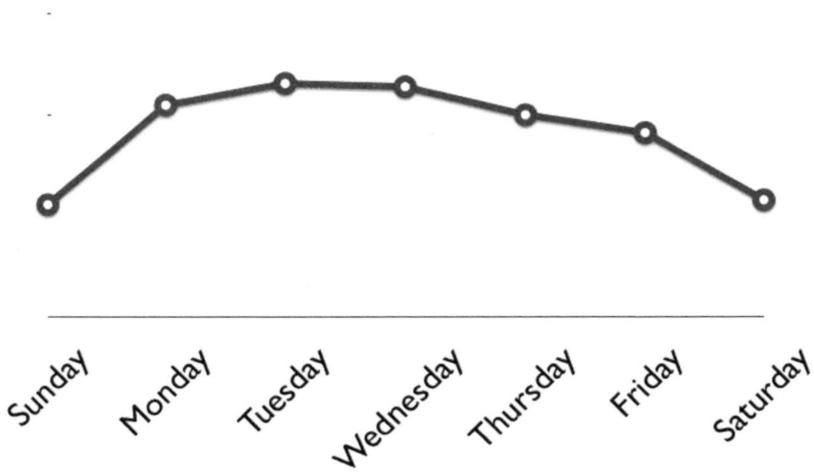

Figure 9: Number of phishing e-mails seen by day of the week

Better indicators that professionalization is underway are in answers to "Who is targeted and when?" As to the "Who?" question, it is where the money is,[6] as shown in Figure 10.

[5] Internet Security Threat Report XI, Symantec Corp.

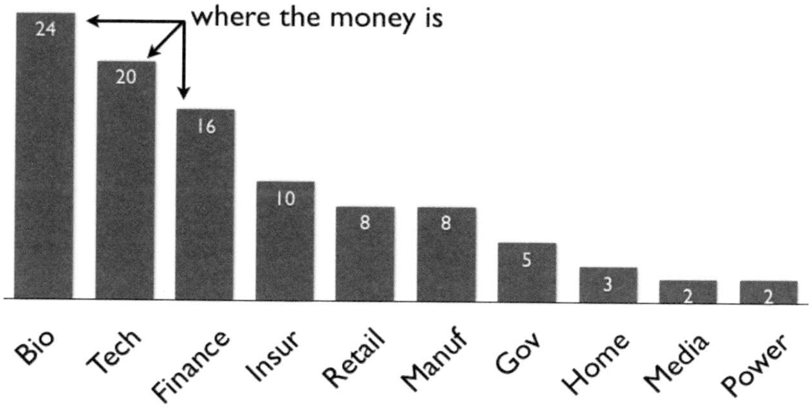

Figure 10: Percent of all data attacks targeted by industrial sector

while as for the "When do they attack?" question, we can see a crescendo of attacks on the Internet Christmas shopper last year (2006) in three ways. First, in Figure 11,[7] there is the rate at which spam e-mail arrives had a substantial rise at that time.

[6] BT/Counterpane, 2007 Attack Trends Report.

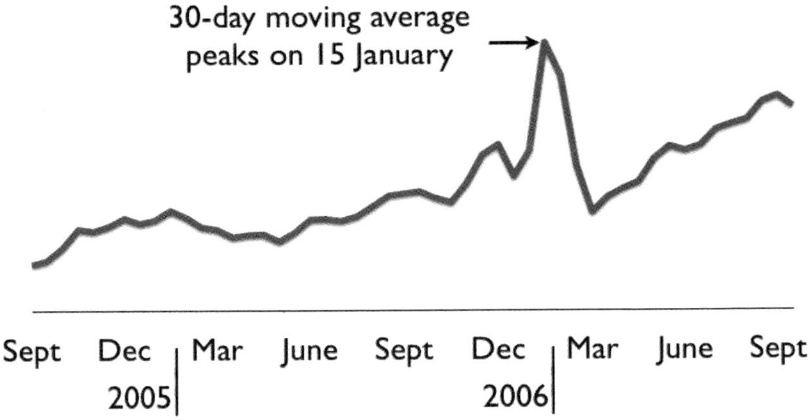

Figure 11: Spam surge at Christmas, 2006

Second, the number of never before detected and thus freshly crafted variants of data-theft malware[8] *attached to that incoming spam e-mail also peaked at that time, as seen in Figure 12 (where discovery and reporting delay is the likely explanation for the peak falling in January of 2007).*

---

[7] Commtouch's online report as available at
www.commtouch.com/Site/ResearchLab/statistics.asp

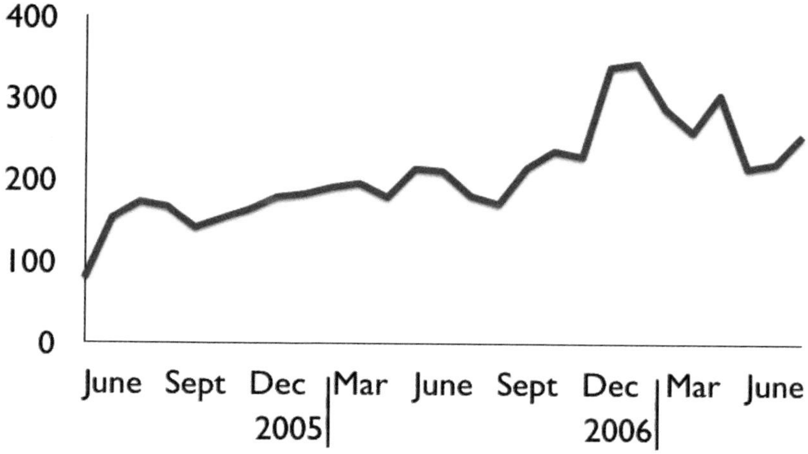

Figure 12: Newly reported data-theft malware in spam, by month

And third, the work factor for data security professionals to defend against known attack methods, as estimated by the National Vulnerability Database,[9] had a near perfect run up at that same time, as seen in Figure 13.

[8] Anti-Phishing Working Group Monthly Report from www.antiphishing.org/reports/apwg_report_july_2007.pdf

Figure 13: Estimated workfactor for information security professionals

The above is overkill if you, the reader, already agree that the opposition is professionalizing, though perhaps these bits of data visualization make it possible to win an argument with skeptical colleagues. Note, however, that if the opposition has indeed professionalized, then the rate of mutation that the attack side can sustain is some orders of magnitude greater than the rate of mutation possible for the amateurs that preceded them. The disparity in sustainable rates arms production between the attack side and the defense side would seem likely to accelerate as the attack side moves to pay for their own R&D out of their own revenues, like any other business. Since the total workload for information security

[9] Published online daily by the National Institute of Standards and Technology; see `nvd.nist.gov/`

professionals is proportional to the cumulative sum of all attack vectors yet invented, but the total work factor for the attack side is proportional to the cost of creating a new attack tool, the professionalization of the attack class punctures the existing security equilibrium by converting the security battlefield from a moderately symmetric one to a highly asymmetric one where the advantage is structurally more favorable to the attackers.

To make concrete these matters of data security in the face of an evolutionary hairpin turn, consider intellectual property protection at, for example, a fab-less chip design firm. Being fab-less keeps down the capital intensity of the firm while, as a tradeoff, concentrating between a quarter and a half of the firm's market capitalization in its R&D pipeline and its know how while requiring both that R&D pipeline and that know how be shared with the actual chip fabs, including prospective downstream partners if the firm is to not become captive to a single such entity. As the present author has said many times, in information-centric industries it is the winners who have the most information in play, it is the losers who have too much, and the line between the most and too much is what security technology exists to draw.

Because such a design firm must be set up to share data with partners more than a firm with in-house fab facilities would, it is natural for intellectual property and like information to be more mobile than it would be in a more monolithic firm. In other words, there will be a lot of people who have a need to share information across the corporate perimeter, enough so that the term "corporate perimeter" largely becomes an oxymoron. In such a setting it does not matter if an internal worker is clumsy, an internal worker has recently been bribed, or the identity of an otherwise competent and honest internal worker has been temporarily taken over by an outside attacker, the effect is the same — internal and valuable information may move to where it should not have gone.

In the face of a professional attack side, the above paragraph takes on a steering role for businesses where the lion's share of corporate value is intellectual property:

To protect intellectual property
you must model the attacker as an insider and
prevention must be your only goal
because secret data is never unrevealed
thus any loss of it is never mitigable.

3. Data security is more business than technical concern

As we think about data security, we admit that it is often more fun and generally more "solvable" to cast it as a technical problem with technical implications, implications for code or silicon or topology. But in actual fact, it is but rarely the case that the technical issues are the ones that matter, or if they matter that they are the point on which real decisions turn. Risk management is where the money is,[10] and risk management is a business concern above all technical concerns of the same name. That goes for liability, revenue protection, conservation of intangible assets, counterparty risk, law enforcement, rules of evidence, compliance, and data's place in disaster recovery regimes. At least those, if not more.

3.1. Liability

The logic here is easy: If (1) the data you hold isn't yours, (2) is valuable to its owner, and (3) you were the one to lose it because you were uncaring, inattentive, disinterested, irresponsible, scatter-brained, feckless, inept, unfit, ineffectual, or just plain mean, then, as your attorney would say, there may be a problem. This book is not the place to review all the precedents (and they vary by jurisdiction, anyway) or to give legal advice,

[10] Geer D, "Risk Management is Where the Money Is," Digital Commerce Society of Boston, 3 November 1998, at: `catless.ncl.ac.uk/risks/20.06.html`

but liability for mishandling data is no longer a theoretic concern but a real concern.

As an example, suppose you do a terrific job of data security within your firm but for real and irresistible business reasons you must use outside firms for some of your functions. This is entirely OK, as illustrated by the fact that unless you're a plumbing supply manufacturer you probably have no business trying to make toilets on your own. Division of labor is what business is all about, and sometimes that division means that some of your work is done on contractual terms. So far, so good.

But with data it is, and seems likely to remain, different. If you take in personally identifiable data from your customers and, for good and valid reasons, you have contract work done on that data (such as to employ an after-hours call center twelve timezones away), then who has reason to complain unless and until your contract call center loses the data you gave them. Your customer will likely say "See you in court" and, of course, your customer will be entirely correct when they say that they gave their data to you, not to somebody else or, as it later turned out, to every thug on the Internet.

Privacy regulations are only one part of this picture, but if the private-data liability risk — which is certainly a business risk rather than a technical one — is proportional to the number of privacy regulations, then the rise in the number of those regulations, shown in Figure 14, makes clear that the potential business risk of liability for data loss cannot be ignored. This is perhaps the most clear example of when a technical risk and a business risk diverge; in truth, if you lose the private customer data to a cat burglar you actually lost a *copy* because you still have it yourself. Technically speaking, you can still go about your business doing the technical things to data that you were expecting to do anyway. Your operational capacity is not diminished by the existence of a second copy — after all, that is what a backup tape is. It is only your business risk that changed.

Data theft is well known and the liability for it is pretty well established already, which actually means that there is a feedback loop in this discussion. You

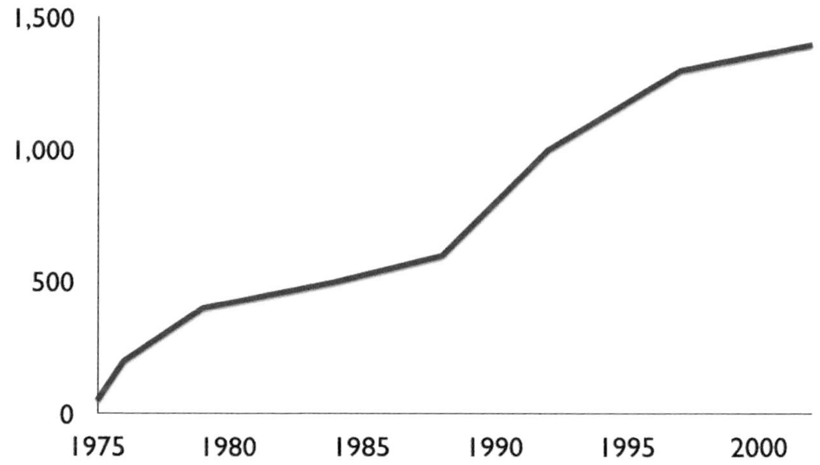

Figure 14: Number of privacy regulations, U.S. Federal + State + Canadian Federal

can't argue that you didn't know data theft was a Bad Thing, so you can't argue that you didn't have some duty to protect against it. You can't argue that you didn't have some duty to protect against data theft, so you can't argue that you shouldn't have known it was going on if it was. You better do something and, perhaps more importantly, be able to prove that you did do something.

3.2. Revenue enhancement and, yes, protection

Historically speaking, it took a long time for the business world's investment in information technology to be traceable all the way through to economic growth at the national level. Now it is obvious in so many ways, contributing to the bottom line on both the cost and the revenue sides of the ledger. The same is true in government, but for this discussion we'll stick to business.

This idea that investment in IT did not bear fruit for a long time and then bore much fruit has been well studied in the academic and policy literature alike, particularly with regard to increases in productivity. From 1973 to 1995, U.S. productivity growth was in a prolonged slowdown, averaging 1.4% *per annum*, whereas for the period 1995-2003 it grew at a remarkable 3.20%. In that latter period of 1995-2003, the amount of capital invested per non-farm worker increased ("deepened") substantially and that investment was largely in information technology. It was only then that gains in productivity per worker could be traced to information technology, *per se*. The share of total U.S. capital expenditures that went for information technology grew from about one percent of GDP in 1960 to about two percent of GDP by 1980 to about three percent of GDP by 1990 to between five and six percent of GDP by 2000. Over that same period, unit prices declined by 4.2% *per annum* for IT in the aggregate and more so for hardware. Figure 15 illustrates this for the entire period 1960-2005 both the steep price declines for IT components relative to price growth in the overall economy and, at the same time, the rising share of customer outlays for IT components as compared to the total dollar value of the GDP itself.[11]

One of the ways in which IT has made business transformation possible is around production efficiencies in manufacturing: the just-in-time control of an entire supply chain, for example. Another is the way in which many firms can have a invisibly cooperative presentation to the end-consumer, as perhaps the travel industry does to the largest degree. Another is the exposure of a far greater percentage of total goods sold to auction pricing, and we don't just mean eBay but also such business to business (B2B) exchanges like Exostar. Yet another is the extension of financial trading to end

---

[11] Adapted from Dale W. Jorgenson's Presidential Address to the American Economic Association, "Information"Technology given in New Orleans, Louisiana on January 6, 2001, as found in Jorgenson's collected papers at:
`post.economics.harvard.edu/faculty/jorgenson/papers` and where the data tables have been updated through 2005 at `AEADATtempAug2006_USWS2005Aug21.pdf` there.

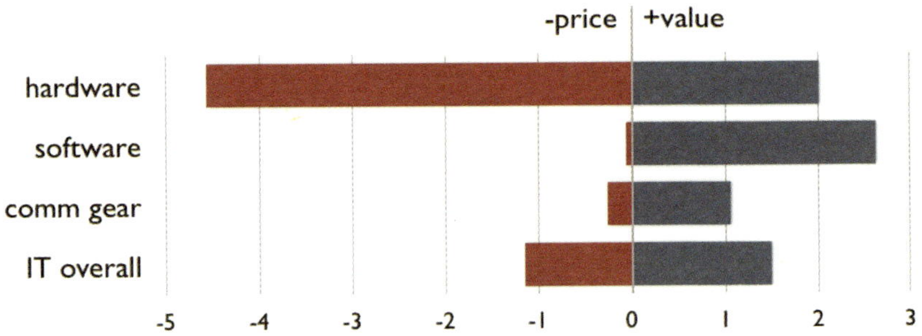

Figure 15: Compound annual grow rates for price and total purchases of IT expressed as multiples of the CAGR for the overall GDP, 1960-2005

users never before reached, and all through the Internet.

In each of these there is real revenue involved or, to be blunt, the IT investment wouldn't have been made or would no longer exist. Just in time efficiencies put money on the bottom line through the revenue side of the ledger as well as the cost side. The travel industry now makes it possible for the end user to pick what it is they want in a way that increases the likelihood that they will actually get up and go somewhere. Auction pricing has made literally thousands of entities with goods able to find and be found by potential counterparties, and to agree on a price — something never before possible. The number of people financially trading, and thus creating transactionally-based revenue for the trading firms, is vast.

All of these examples and more require data security to function, and without data security they simply fail. You can't get just in time delivery if data poisoning happens. You can't book travel if the data is poisoned or anything other than 100% available. You can't have an auction if any part of the data supporting it is subject to manipulation or even otherwise valid data is delayed in its presentation. You certainly can't have trading if the data involved is subject to early release to other parties, financial details get in the wrong hands, or counterparties are misidentified to one or the other's advantage.

These are just examples, but it is hard to imagine any "electronic commerce" enterprise where data security isn't just about paramount. This may mean avoiding data theft, it may mean avoiding data poisoning, and it may mean avoiding the loss of data availability. In the examples and more, data security is why there is revenue those industries can count on, and a loss of data security would cost them revenue. If any firm has not yet faced up to the fact their data makes their revenue possible needs to re-think, and soon. Ask yourself: If the company's disaster recovery (DR) plan doesn't include the company's data as a component as critical, if not more so, than its physical plant, then why? There better be a good answer.

3.3. Conservation of intangible assets

The duties of any company's top executives are to grow the company's shareholder value, just as the duty of any company's Board of Directors is to (select the officers who will) protect the company's assets. For the most important sorts of decisions, committing to entirely new markets, mergers and acquisitions, divestitures and spin-offs, and so forth generally involve the power of the Board to advise and consent to that which the executive proposes, with the Board representing those who own the firm and whose assets are thus at risk to any considerable action by the executive. (That this is a mirror to some forms of government is noted but held irrelevant to the points now being made.)

This protection of assets as a duty is a considerable one, not the least of which is that simply saying "No" to any novel proposal is not what protection of assets means. In business, the company that is not moving forward is likely moving backward, *i.e.*, initiatives and their attendant risk are a necessity. In some sense, both a CEO wanting to take a company in a new direction and a Board wanting to put less at risk than does the CEO are both exercising a kind of skepticism that is healthy.

What has changed, however, of the past few years is a remarkable re-balancing of the ratio of tangible to intangible assets. Not so very long ago, and certainly with the scope of the career of nearly all who sit on Boards of Directors, intangible assets would be few and the value would not be anything like a majority of the company's net worth. This is no longer so certain.

Intangible assets are non-monetary assets (cannot be seen or touched) created at the cost of time and/or effort. There two kinds: (1) legal intangibles such as trade secrets like customer lists, copyrights to created works, patents both as to the intellectual property they describe and the market advantage they confer, trade- and servicemarks, and the slipperiest of all, goodwill, and (2) competitive intangibles like know-how, collaborative agreements, leverage however defined, and structural advantages. Legal intangibles are property rights and are defensible in a court of law as anything owned would be. Competitive intangibles are not property rights, though they can and do modify the cost-effectiveness, productivity, and opportunity costs of the enterprise. Competitive intangibles can nevertheless effect revenue and costs, customer satisfaction, public perception and, in particular, that part of the market value of the firm due to public perception. Some would say that for most firms, the sum of its personnel is a competitive intangible — or could be — and, in any case, competitive advantage is what competitive intangibles are all about.

Because these matters bear on the duties and responsibilities of the firm, it is no wonder that the (U.S.) Uniform Commercial Code, UCC Section 9-102(a)(42), has a definition:

> General intangibles are any personal property ... other than accounts, chattel paper, commercial tort claims, deposit accounts, documents, goods, instruments, investment property, letter of credit rights, letters of credit, money, and oil, gas, or other minerals before extraction. The term includes payment intangibles and software.

The point we are making here is this: Data is clearly an intangible asset in and of itself and, in some cases which can be read between the lines above, were it not for data security the intangible asset would cease being an asset at all. Perhaps nowhere else is it so true that the value of data is due to the security of it, or that data without security can have no value.

Though we won't go into it here, the U.S. Financial Accounting Standards Board (FASB), a private sector entity, defines how an intangible asset is recognized on the books and records of the firm. Another Anglophone democracy, Australia, has the corresponding Australian Accounting Standards Board (AASB), a public sector entity, and the AASB is considering a change in accounting practices that would require all intangible assets to be listed on the corporate balance sheet. This is nothing so much as the culmination of prophecy, *viz.*,

> Some day, on the corporate balance sheet, there will be an entry which reads, "Information," for in most cases the information is more valuable than the hardware which processes it.
> — Adm. Grace Murray Hopper, U.S. Navy, 1987

though, for the most forward thinking executives, it will

be merely the rest of the world catching up:

> The information about the packages we ship is more valuable than the packages themselves.
> — Fred Smith, Federal Express, *ca.* 1990

This change in accounting standards, if it transpires, would make a very important statement to those of us who worry with data security, *viz.*, that to be an accounted-for asset means there is a value that must be associated with it and that as a balance sheet item the Boards of Directors of all listed firms would answer to misuse of the corporate asset that data represents.

In the first case, we who do security metrics entirely too often find that a promising line of inquiry comes to naught over the complete absence of any believable number for "How much is this data worth?" We may approximate the wished-for answer with a replacement value (what would it cost to create again from scratch), a black market price (so many examples, so little time), the future economic value of data now in hand (such as a biotech patent application in progress but still secret), or just the ugly lower bound gotten by dividing the enterprise's IT budget by the raw volume of its data (arriving at a price per bit). If accounting standards step into this breach, we may soon have a set of real numbers to play with. That this transition might be painful reminds one of nothing so much as the U.S. Marine's "Pain is weakness leaving the body."

In the second case, once data has a value and once that value appears on the balance sheet, then the interplay between the Boards of Directors and the CEOs of this world will include, amongst the other valuations to be protected and to be grown, the valuation of data. It is not hard to imagine that near deadlocks in Boardrooms of the near-term future will be broken by the calculus of data security risk as much as they have heretofore been broken by the calculus of asset risk of any other sort long recognized. This area of ferment bears watching or, for firms who prefer to be ready before the need to be ready presents itself head-on, it may be time to make-ready for a financial regime that prices data and hence data security, and to do so quite soon now. Being ahead of the curve will not be an option, in this observer's view, for very much longer, so this seems like a good time to again look at how this works out in practice; an example follows.

One of the clearest examples of data that has value is data held on behalf of customers of the firm. Turning to the dictionary, the customer entrusts his data with the firm, which is to say he puts his data into the firm's care, and also intrusts his data to the firm, which is to say confers a trust upon the firm as formalized by the transfer of his data to it.

Repeating the above, the past few years have seen the extension of financial trading to end users never before reached, and all through the Internet, with the common understanding that you can't have trading if the data involved is subject to early release to other parties, financial details get in the wrong hands, or counterparties are misidentified to one or the other's advantage. As such, the customer's act of entrusting his data with the firm and intrusting his data to the firm, clearly both transfers value and, ultimately, creates value all of which is held in the form of data and neither bullion nor certificates.

Due to regulatory requirements, trading firms record much data about data, including all communications between the firm and its clients, purely digital communications or otherwise, and retains these for (typically) seven (7) years. One might also observe that the more authority a member of the trading firm's staff has, the greater the likelihood that their own use of data is on some sort of device that is portable if not pocket-sized, and network connected, if only intermittently. No one within the firm will deny that all this data, original customer data, data incidentally thrown off by the process of making money, and/or data about data communications, has value because no one now employed is likely to know how to operate without it.

So what is a financial firm to do? Play to its existing strengths, that's what. All such firms understand that risk has a target value and that that target value is non-zero. In trading strategies, insufficient risk taking means leaving money on the table for competitors and existing customers will be hearing from those competitors when the quarterly yield numbers are calculated. Excess risk taking, by contrast, is eventually self limiting as excess risk tends to accumulate and may ultimately exceed reserves. Risk is not anathema in and of itself; well understood risk is a dial to adjust. This is what the finance side of the house knows, and that is the strength to play to.

In the case of data risk, however, we do not have the models, the actuarial tail, or the simulation platforms that we have in finance. The models can be gotten, and they need not be all that complex so long as some classification of data as to its upside value and its downside threat can be done. The actuarial tail will be a continuing challenge as the constant rate of change makes the collection of risk versus outcome data to four digits of accuracy nearly impossible — in contrast to, say, life insurance. The simulation platforms may be possible; certainly there are parallels to what-if financial models when penetration tests are done, just as there are parallels to leading economic indicators in automated collection of accurate network dependency diagrams. Note, however, that to build a simulation platform for data risk without the knowledge of what data the firm has would be silly.

If the firm were starting from a known state, good or otherwise, its data model could be based on location of data — a state diagram as an engineer might think of it. A state diagram has transitions and, in turn, the knowledge about data risk would then be of the form "If transition X can occur while in state Y, then it is worth spending Z to prevent that from happening." This may involve many estimates, but at least it permits a classification of states as to whether their data situation is better of worse and, if worse, what avoiding that worsening is worth. We discuss this further in the chapter on security metrics, but state diagram transitions are what reliability calculations are made of and it is likely that, for a financial firm, much labor has already been expended to understand the reliability of corporate IT where, as with data, not all transitions are fully understood but knowing which state to prefer is straightforward.

But, to be realistic, let's presume that we are not starting from a known state. In such a situation, we likely do not know how data moves and our first action would be start recording how data moves across the board so as to build a model of data movement in lieu of a model of total data state. In a sense, this is parallel to what intrusion prevention systems do — being preloaded or having learned what patterns of behavior are ordinary, they call attention to those which are not ordinary. This focus on the anomalous is precisely what you do when you don't know everything but you do know something. Putting aside the problems of false positive alarm conditions, this works well enough to be in widespread use. The parallel can be done with data; but first the firm must come to some conclusion as to what are ordinary data movements and thus what are extraordinary ones.

A data surveillance regime set to "record" only, i.e., not to intervene but merely to watch, is a first step. Some data movements are sure to be known-bad without any need to sample, such as writing customer data to USB devices or printing screen shots of design plans, and with suitable technology those can be blocked outright, but it is our experience that real knowledge of how data moves is very much not the norm, and thus the first priority for the firm is to get a handle on what is normal. Of course, knowing what is of value, such as through a formal data classification exercise, is the gold standard, and that should be the preferred long-term outcome for any firm, but just as with network traffic, until you know precisely what it is that must be permitted, it is best to get a handle on what is present so that "deny" decisions become possible. Put differently, when you know nothing permit-all is the only option. When you know something, default-permit is what you can and should do. When you know everything, default-deny becomes possible, and only then.

3.4. Counterparty risk as a business issue

Everyone knows that the idea of outsourcing is part of what sustains growth at the global level. There are no firms which can afford to simply ignore the cost differentials in a world shrunken by network communications and the logistics they make possible. They may choose not to avail themselves of those cost differentials, but they must examine them even if the outsourcing is entirely within the network neighborhood.

Firms that do put together contracts with other firms that do some part of the total business better or at better cost than the home firm does, have a question they should ask themselves: Is the data they must share with the outsourcer as safe with that outsourcer as it was with the home firm? If as good or better, then wonderful. If not as good, is that reflected in the price?

Put differently, the better the job your firm does at data security the more the remaining risk you hold is counterparty risk. This is no surprise: If we cured cancer tomorrow the proportion of death due to heart disease would climb. Perhaps, then, the issue of counterparty risk is of unique importance to firms doing a basic good job at data security since by doing a good job they exhaust the areas of action where they hold command power.

Or maybe they don't. Maybe the data security issues are now so important that they merit contractual language. Certainly the credit card associations (like Mastercard and VISA) think that they do merit contractual language that is effectively the imposition of private law. Credit card associations are more insistent and penetrating than "official" regulators since, as regulators but not public bodies, they have the ability to enforce rather strongly such things as the Payment Card Industry (PCI) standards.[12]

That idea of private law in the form of contractual agreements is spreading. In outsourced situations like call centers in Central America or design centers in Beijing or trading centers in Hong Kong or back offices in Mumbai, no firm can rely on anything but the ability to enforce contracts. This is not an insult to any sovereign nation who might take offense at having their laws and law enforcement described as irrelevant, but it doesn't matter whether the laws or the law enforcers are competent or not. The enterprise that puts its data in jurisdictions where it exercises little to no influence has but a few strategies for keeping that data where it belongs, and those strategies are variations on one theme: Make the business relationship contingent on compliance with contractual rules, make those rules carry serious

---

[12] For the barest introduction, see usa.visa.com/merchants/risk_management/cisp_merchants.html

penalties, and have enough built-in surveillance that bypassing the rules, while perhaps still possible, cannot be silent.

The demands of outsourcing relationships are themselves all variations on the theme of "How do I get service as good as I can myself provide at lower cost but without losing control?" In that sense, data security is simply another species of the need for control. Yet, at the same time, because of the unique characteristics of data, *viz.*, that it leaves no vacuum when stolen, theft occurs at the speed of light, and once gone there is no getting it back, the importance of prevention over mitigation is nowhere else as great as it is with the firm's data. Building's can be rebuilt, but when "the firm's data" actually means "our customer's data that was entrusted to us," the importance of prevention over mitigation is underlined.

The kinds of preventative controls available include ones that severely limit the usefulness of data, such as purpose-built buildings with only one satellite link to the home office, no printers, and all the USB ports sealed with a glue gun. These make data less useful, so the cost savings had better be truly substantial else the tradeoff between capability and cost will be much less attractive on close examination than on first blush. Better, it would seem, to make the data as useful as it is possible to make it, but to have mechanisms that, despite the usability of the data, still prevent it from moving out of the envelope of protection. This is the very embodiment of that perennial challenge to security technology: to be enabling.

These mechanisms amount to surveillance, and there is no point in beating around the bush about such a word. In this sense, the factory time clock is a surveillance tool as well, just as the card-key entry lock or, for a stronger example, the requirement that those who work for investment banks must have all their investments with that bank so that their own trade activity is automatically watched. Though we will talk of it later, the core message for the business leader is simple: Because of the special characteristics of data, if you don't watch it then you won't have it. With the proliferation of counterparties, watching it takes on rather special meaning and particularly special where technical surveillance is the only tool you have absent the rule of law in a court of competent jurisdiction, and even courts cannot unwind time. Let's again pause to illustrate these points with two examples.

The first example might be called inherent or structural outsourcing and we'll use the health care industry as a point of discussion. Health information and the privacy of it is a regulated matter, and one which illustrates that having the most information in play is very close to having too much information in play. You, as a consumer and/or patient, want to control your health information, but you probably also want it readily available to others when you are unconscious and in need of urgent care. Perhaps no other area so well illustrates that the logical price of ready availability is not ever more detailed access control but rather ever more certain accountability.

However, medicine is a place uniquely rich in counterparties: hospitals, private care physicians, clinical groups including whole departments in some hospitals, outpatient facilities that are siphoning off day surgery and other such aspects of care, home health care agencies, and so forth and so on. It is also a place where the useful lifetime of data is perhaps the longest.

This is not the place to dissect the Health Information Portability & Accountability Act (HIPAA), except perhaps to look at the name of the statute and see that it echoes the idea that data, to be useful, has to move and yet despite moving has to be safe. If ever there was a conclusion built into a name, then this is it.

Another aspect of health information is that all parties to it are as likely to write as to read, i.e., there is no "master-slave" relationship between producers and consumers of health data and so synchronization of the current health record is many-to-many synchronization, not one to many. In such a circumstance, accountability is almost the only idea that can be imagined working.

Health providers are driven by events — you show up with a broken arm wherever the nearest emergency room is — and they can work with less than perfect information because they must. In parallel, data protection in the health industry is also event driven because data is created when care is delivered. This means that a data protection regime for health information must be distributed, have some common language for establishing veracity of that information, and be traceable to its source. As with finance, this tends to make it ultimately cost effective to record all health information not only as to what the value of some indicium, but also as to the entire context in which the health data was collected.

The end consumer of health related services of all types cares deeply about the outcome. For better or worse, this sometimes manifests itself in medical malpractice litigation. Because the medical systems of first world countries are ever more data driven, there will be times when the validity and sanctity of health data become part of court cases. Being able to prove that such and such a bit of health data was or was not presented to the caregiver at such and such a time is often was is effectively meant when the question, "Given what was known, was this care competent and warranted?"

As with other settings mentioned in this book, such a question can occasionally turn on proving a negative. As science teaches us, proving a negative is impossible except in the case where all possible alternatives are known and each is examined. When it comes to the protection and logging of health information, any subsequent litigation that may reference the "What did they know and when did they know it?" questions will come to require that a negative occasionally be proved. Only when all health information is captured and all the metadata about the context in which that health information was captured is itself also captured will be able to frankly answer such questions. The design or upgrade of health information systems must recognize the new requirements and constraints that these observations imply.

The second example of an industrial outsourcing area with data security inherent to it is best illustrated by looking at a provider of services to which other firms outsource their internal functions. Because of the cost-driven selling proposition of most outsource firms, the way in which data is handled ends up being a marker for where data security has to be integrated. For a small but coherent example, consider call centers where call center staff are employees working out of their homes (a.k.a. "home agents"). This is not something that, per se, the outsource firm wishes to call attention to, but to avoid calling attention to it means that data protections had better be really quite good and auditably so. Because outsource firms naturally mix the data of all of those who contract with them, and because outsource firms will almost surely have several lines of business, the data surveillance is almost surely divorced from the data control function in the sense that at the enterprise level a decision to require data surveillance firm-wide is prudent and necessary, but the particular mitigations and controls are almost surely unique to the lines of business.

Such a central mandate to make data security visible coupled to a divisional level decision process over what that which is visible translates into action as, seems the best of all worlds. The central authority can do risk analytics based on information whose method and consistency of collection they know and control while the divisional authority can decide what level of risk and countermeasure it wishes to field. The amount of risk the firm can hold is always larger when there is zero ambiguity over who holds what part of that risk, while remembering that security is a means rather than and end requires that risk taking decisions be as close to the front lines as possible.

3.5. Law enforcement and rules of evidence

Since December, 2006, the U.S. Rules of Civil Procedure have made proving the trustworthiness of data a central issue before any data can be admitted as evidence, and that means lifecycle trustworthiness. The courts are, in this way, facing facts even if they are somewhat late in doing so. The fact they are facing in particular is that while a person may swear to speak the truth, the whole truth, and nothing but the truth, data is data and therefore without knowing the manner in which the data was collected, handled, protected, and retained that that data must be assumed suspect. Where people are innocent until proven guilty, data is contrariwise unbelievable until proven that it should be believed.

This change has a trendy name, "E-Discovery," and like all changes in court matters the full impact will not be evident for some time until case law develops. It is, however, well documented[13] The trendy name implies most of what this is about, namely a change in how discovery motions are scoped and complied with when the discovery is aimed at electronic data.

Whole tomes have already been written on what this means for you, and it is not the place of this book to either reproduce those or to give legal advice. We can, however, say that there is no doubt now that just saying

---

[13] Amendments to the Federal Rules of Civil Procedure, as found officially at `www.uscourts.gov/rules/EDiscovery_w_Notes.pdf`

"You wanted my data, here is all that I have" is no longer even halfway to the goal. You will have to prove, not assert as you would with your own personal testimony, that the data represents the whole truth and nothing but the truth. Depending on the tenaciousness of opposing counsel and the viewpoints of the judge, this may be real work, real work for which preparation will pay dividends like no other.

In criminal matters the changes are less clear, which is to say that a direct set of rule changes as referred to above don't exist. Case law is, however, setting precedent. Not all of this is pleasant, but in any case just having data without being able to show the provenance of that data over a wide range of potential challenges to it will leave one side or the other in a world of hurt.

Perhaps the most extreme example, and one would hope an example entirely irrelevant to the readers of this book other than as a matter which they should understand, consider the U.S. Ninth Circuit Court of Appeals (California) whose decision in the "Free Speech Coalition *v.* Reno" case found that the visual depiction of child pornography is protected speech unless it can be shown that the child in question is real and identifiable — after all, it might be a virtual child.[14] In other words, if you cannot prove that what is in the picture is

[14] Free Speech Coalition v. Reno, 198 F.3d 1083, 1086 (9th Cir. 1999) as found at caselaw.lp.findlaw.com/scripts/getcase.pl?court=9th&navby=case&no=9716536o&exact=1

a real child (by producing that child), then the assumption is that the picture is "a lie."

Returning to civil matters, the Zubulake decision[15] sets precedents about even data retention. Again, it is not the place of this book to dissect that case but the message is reinforcing that data you have had better be data that you can show is the whole truth. Zubulake demonstrated that when you cannot show that data you have is the whole truth, you will be at risk of adverse jury instructions from the judge. That is what happened in Zubulake and it involved nothing more than an inability on the part of UBS Warburg to produce e-mail demanded under discovery as, depending on the version of events depicted by opposing counsels, the e-mail had been routinely destroyed or intentionally lost.

The data retention question, how much to keep and for how long, is a serious one. What you keep must, as a business reality, be kept in such a way that it retains its potential evidentiary quality; that much is certain. What remains uncertain, and is thus for you and your General Counsel to work out, is whether retaining everything is the safest path or whether destruction by the clock is better (bearing in mind that what you destroy will be questioned if you have reason to believe that anyone would ever want to demand that you produce it).

---

[15] Zubulake v. UBS Warburg LLC, 220 F.R.D. 212, 216 (S.D. N.Y. 2003), as found at `www.nysd.uscourts.gov/rulings/02cv01243_072403.pdf`

These are not easy questions, and they come with a large number of unanticipatables. The boundary between risk aversion and prudence is unmarked, but as a business this is perhaps a place where you must make decisions. As the cliché of the 1960s had it, "Not to decide is to decide." At the very least, avoiding answering "I don't know" under oath is to be avoided.

3.6. Compliance

Nearly no one reading this book hasn't already experienced the cost and deadline pressure of some form of regulatory compliance. There is no need to just retell that, and, besides, nearly all forms of compliance pressure are specific to the industry vertical, *e.g.*, privacy regulations in and around health care, transparency regulations in and around financial services, health and safety regulations all over, and so forth. Nevertheless, it is perhaps important to note that nearly everything involving compliance ends up involving acquiring and preserving records at varying degrees of specificity and for varying periods of time. As this is the first decade of the 21st century, those records are electronic data, and they come with risk of their own.

First are the downside costs of failing to maintain the availability of those records. While touched on in the next section, availability is a pre-condition for the use of compliance records in whatever procedure to which they may later be put. (Not available? May as well not exist.)

Second are the downside costs of failing to maintain the integrity of those records. This is clearly a data security issue, *per se*. Integrity of records is not complicated to achieve so long as the need for it is anticipated, excepting in the particular circumstance of an attack on record integrity by someone with natural authority over the storage mechanisms themselves. This tends to mean IT workers with authority, though it can also additionally include staff in accounting, personnel, and legal. As a design goal, any data security regime should assume that authority, like power, tends to corrupt and that unchecked authority, like absolute power, tends to do so with certainty. As such, designers of data security regimes might want to imagine a turncoat within and organize their thoughts around that; if the resulting design can withstand a turncoat then it can likely withstand other threats. Putting this in compliance terms, if you can look opposing counsel (or a Judge) in the eye and say that "not even the CFO can override the records here" or the like, then in fact you have something you can bank a lot on.

Third are the downside costs of failing to acquire operational data at all. In the case of information security compliance, which after all is what underlies nearly everything from (the United States') HIPAA, Sarbanes-Oxley, Gramm-Leach-Bliley, *etc.*, the risk can perhaps be stated as "should have known but did not" and this maps directly not to a failure to acquire but a failure to fully acquire. This is the heart of the Civil Procedure issue discussed just above — is the data presented to the

Court or Regulator complete (the whole truth)? If not, and in particular if your side cannot deflect a charge by opposing counsel that your submission into evidence of electronic records is a carefully chosen, inherently favorable subset of all records, then you will clearly have difficulty prevailing.

While the regulatory burden is idiosyncratic to particular verticals (proving that your trucking company's drivers get regular physicals, say), the data handling after acquisition is likely to be a commonality across various industries, and neatly summed up by the classic CIA rule: Confidentiality, Integrity, and Availability. Therefore, a general data security regime that has CIA characteristics is one that can keep compliance data in good enough shape to survive challenge.

Therefore let us turn to the specific case of compliance data acquisition. For some industries, this is not relevant, but from this observer's vantage it appears that all physical and analog sources of data are converted to digital form as quickly as possible. However, when the source information is itself digital, such as limiting who has "write" access to a medical record, there is a special character to the compliance question inasmuch as the act of enforcing policy is the one and only place to acquire (and retain) proof that policy was enforced. It is one thing to say that fire extinguishers must be re-charged every N months as a chart on the wall, the records at the fire services firm, and a gauge on the fire extinguisher all tell versions of the same fact — re-charge was recent enough that the extinguisher is (and can be seen to be) in working order.

By contrast, if the regulatory burden is about data handling, then it is factually impossible to ensure compliance unless the records are derived from the enforcement at the instant of the application of that enforcement. Put differently, because of the peculiar characteristics of digital data unless the enforcement is at the point of use of that data then the compliance records about whether enforcement happened are worthless. As described elsewhere, your data can be stolen and yet you will still have it. Your programs or keyboard can be bugged and yet your keyboard and programs will still work. Your assurances to regulators will be in complete good faith and will have no basis in fact, only hope. Unless data, and the handling of data, is under some kind of pervasive surveillance, your statements will be probabilistic rather than deterministic. Regulators are not always able to be this subtle.

3.7. Data's place in disaster recovery regimes

Every substantial firm has a reliability requirement for some part of its operations. For some, like electric power or banking, the reliability requirements are both easy to understand and the subject of regulation. For others, like factories with a full pipeline, the requirements are just as real but less obvious unless closely examined. All firms with a reliability requirement must, if they are to have a long-term future, consider what to level of disaster they might be exposed and to what degree enduring such a disaster requires current investment.

Oftimes, a disaster recovery plan involves two principal components: the ability to operate at reduced levels of productivity and the ability to return to pre-disaster levels without having to invent every single step under fire. With the utmost humility and reverence for that which was lost, let us consider the biggest "natural experiment" in recent memory, the September 11, 2001, felling of the World Trade Center in New York City.

Calling this a natural experiment is an awkward construction, but for the purpose of learning from it that is what it was. We will not name the banks in question, but we will not fabricate details, either. In the first case, one bank had dispersed both its people and its computing resources such that disaster prevention was accomplished by not having a single point of failure. That bank did survive the event and even contributed some of its facilities to the others which fared not so well.

Another bank had dispersed its computing resources but had localized its staff so that communications between them were as good as those communications could be. In part, this had included have a single telephone exchange that rang only to this bank, thus effectively outsourcing a portion of the communications structure of the bank to the much more capable telephony provider of record. As that telephony provider suffered the loss of an entire switching center, the switching center that included the bank's telephone exchange, what was a survivable disaster for the telephony provider was a much bigger disaster for the bank. Had not the application of extraordinary funds and receiving the aid of what on other days were competitors both been possible, this bank might have had an irrecoverable failure.

The third bank had chosen a redundancy path that involved having two data centers, each with separate communications, separate power providers, separate staff, and so forth, but placed one in WTC-1 and the other in WTC-2. The logic was appealing: Should one of these two redundant data centers be lost, by having the other — supplied with different comms, different power, *etc.* — as close as the adjacent building the bank would absolutely maximize the availability of extra staff to whichever of the two data centers became the fall-back to the other. What, of course, happened is that not one but two disasters befell this bank and, as such, they turned out to have little disaster recovery capability at all. Again, had it not been for otherwise competitors to provide clearing services for this bank, it would have been a formal bank failure (in the language of banks) and would not be in business today.

We say all this not to fetishize the events of that day, world-changing though they were, but to make clear that a disaster recovery plan can be very good by accident and very bad, also by accident. There are costs associated with spending on disaster preparedness that will never be made up if no disaster occurs. We all likely know an individual who drives like hell, never wears a seatbelt, and is still on the planet. Your firm can do the same, if it likes, but it will not be thought prudent.

With data, then, what is prudent and what is the relevance of any discussion of disaster recovery to the themes of this book? That is actually rather simple: The ability of most firms to operate is long since dependent on the movement of and access to data. That data is firm-specific, part evanescent and part quite stable. The thought experiment of saying "What if all my data, and only my data, were to disappear overnight?" will get you in the right frame of mind to consider these questions.

Clearly, redundancy is helpful, though you must always remember that if the disaster is the intentional infliction of remotely based attacks on you, then if all your computers carry the same vulnerabilities that increased redundancy will actually increase your risk, not lower it. Clearly, dispersion is helpful, though you must likewise remember that without comms to coordinate dispersed resources they will diverge (think about re-synchronizing databases that have been allowed to take on new entries while disconnected). Clearly, diminished operation can be as helpful to a firm as anesthesia is to a surgical patient — keep the important stuff going and turn off the unimportant.

All of these require thought, and that thought is best done when the klaxons & strobes are not doing their thing. This means that you need to understand what data resources are essential and what are not, just as you need to understand what staff are essential and what are not. It means charting a path between costs you hope never to recover, and costs you hope never to bear. With data, you have an advantage that you do not have with machine tools or office furniture — the second copy has zero capital cost and thus only an operational cost. Spare capacity that is used (and not just sitting idle like a backup diesel generator) is the best way to insure that your data works and will work when other things don't. The other thought experiment might instead be "What if my data, and only my data, were to still be here tomorrow?" For that data that makes recovery possible, you've no choice but to ensure that it makes it.

At the outset we suggested that, as we think about data security, it is more fun and more solvable to cast it as a technical problem with technical implications, implications for code or silicon or topology. But in actual fact, the technical issues are not the ones that matter. Risk management in a data-rich world is still first and foremost a business concern even if the nature of data contravenes all our intuitions about what is an asset, what is liability, what it means to protect revenue, who has to worry with the conservation of intangible assets, how counterparty risk eventually dominates any data security regime, where our friends in the law stand (and sit), and data's place in disaster recovery regimes.

These are business questions;
they are about ends.
Technical matters are about means.
Never confuse the two.

4. Solutions begin with choice

Choice. The problem is choice. Solutions themselves begin and end with choice. Few of them are pretty. Some of these include choosing between an incremental reform strategy versus a big-bang strategy, the apparent regulatory need to prove a negative versus, or in addition to, the security need just to recognize that which is itself negative, the choices that differentiate treating data security as a tax versus as an investment, and even whether the asymmetric war we are in is worth winning versus whether just diverting attacks to others is good enough. All are against the axiomatic backdrop that data security is a means, not an end, and that we must avoid letting the best be the enemy of the good. The high point of this discussion will be how much of security thought today is a generalized risk management approach and how much it it is not, how different security for data is from security for candy bars, train cars, or movie stars.

As we think about data protection, which is to say when we think about any digital security question at all, we have to make choices and those choices embody the universal truth that all security is about tradeoffs. This is not a new thought, but it is easy to forget. If you happen to read the hard-core security mailing lists, you will know that nearly every discussion will occasionally veer off into an argument that can only be characterized as "the Best is the enemy of the Good."

That is not what we want. What we want is what Sandhu called "Good enough security"[16]

> Good enough is good enough
> Good enough always beats perfect
> The really hard part is determining what
> is good enough

This is why we are here today.

4.1. The incremental reform strategy *vs.* the big-bang strategy

There are many situations in life where one asks "Is this worth fixing, or should I just start over?" In most of those situations where the decision is difficult, the reason it is difficult is a matter of tradeoffs. On the one hand will be continuity, familiarity, and minimization of incremental cost in the short term. On the other hand will be minimization of cost over the long term, the possibility of enabling more than just a solution to the present danger, and the chance to shed some of the baggage that always accompanies continuity. There is nothing special about security in this regard — it is, after all, entirely about tradeoffs and, which is more, because security is a means and not an end, the true costs of any security solution will be dominated by integration and the true benefits will be dominated by a

[16] Sandhu R: "Good-Enough Security: Toward a Pragmatic Business-Driven Discipline," IEEE Internet Computing, January/February 2003, v5 n3 p66.

freedom of motion not otherwise obtainable.

When looking at data security initiatives in this light, it is perhaps obvious to the reader how other of life's "Is it worth fixing, or should I just start over?" maps to the problems with which the term "data security" concerns itself. It is patently true that new threats show up relatively often. Sometime they are variations on a theme, such as the rate at which viruses mutate, and sometimes wholly new threats, such as rootkits with anti-forensic capabilities.[17]

Internet-time being as fast as it is, it is easy to forget how fast new threats appear. The value of data being as it is (and is becoming), it is also easy to forget just how much value can walk away. Because of how fast the clock runs, each new threat comes on more like a thunderclap than a rising tide, it is entirely natural and almost entirely rational to solve problems one at a time. It may be all that you can do.

Too, the incremental appeals to folks who want to treat security as a reactive discipline. A new threat has arrived? Not to worry, technicians are crafting a new shield even now. You are worried about USB tokens that can hold all the payroll records and still be something the opponent can slip into a wallet or a more intimate location? Well, then, here is a product that blocks writes to USB tokens, perhaps even with a little logic

[17] "Anti-forensic" means that not only is the hidden code hard to find, but it covers its tracks such that it is harder still even after the fact.

about what might still be OK. You are worried that peer-to-peer (P2P) applications can not only carry attachments but encrypt them, too? Well, then, let's add a new set of firewall rules. You are worried that wireless networks advertise their weaknesses? Well, why don't you go through the drill of making all wireless connections require the best security protocols, never allow connection to out-of-company access points except to initiate a VPN connection to home base, and maybe even skip 802.11 entirely by opting for the cell networks. You are worried that malware mutates? Then by all means, sign up for automatic update of every signature-based system you own. Worried that a rogue device can be carried into your inner sanctum and bypass the network perimeter? Perhaps it is time to buy all new routers and deploy Cisco's NAC or something of the sort.

It is endless. In fact, that is the point: It is endless. This is not good news, but for any firm where reliability is a top tier requirement, not breaking things will be the embodiment of that top tier requirement so making the smallest change that can cure the current threat makes a lot of sense. It can even position you as a leader — after all, don't leaders have one of everything? Of course they do. That is nearly the only way to stay abreast of the wave of threat in real time — buy one of everything the minute it appears.

By contrast, a big bang approach is the dream of every reformer. No socialist (non-)paradise has ever incrementally mutated itself into a free market. Sure,

China is trying to do just that, but even the iconic Mao Tse Tung said that to make an omelette you have to break some eggs. If you want to get ahead of the threat, then you have to get ahead of the threat. You can't be reactive since, by simple definition, if you are reactive the threat comes to you. No, if you want to get ahead of the threat you have to either invest more than the opponent does, you have to be a fortune teller, or you have to understand that when you are losing a game you cannot afford to lose, then you have to change the rules.

A big bang strategy is like that. It isn't tried often, and a lot of times when it is tried it is because some public embarrassment of the first order has made all the arguments for incrementalism and caution seem like so much dodging. There is no need to rehash (and re-embarrass) the firms involved in big losses of data security over the past five years, but all those that have survived have changed the way they do business, making data security a job that actually does trump other jobs. Perhaps that is the only way that a big bang can happen in a large firm — maybe breaching a dam is the only way to clear the river channel. Maybe, as with politics, reform is only possible when driven by crisis. No one wishes for the circumstance of a big loss out of the blue — no one — but if one does happen, then it is the true leader who actually does take the crisis and mold it into an opportunity.

4.2. Proving a negative *vs.* recognizing the negative

A lot of security solutions start with some sort of detection mechanism, some sort of trip wire or see-in-the-dark glasses that can yell "there it is" when a problem is still small enough to block. This is itself entirely natural — the threats we face cannot be caught with the human eye; they are too many, too hard to see, too fast. Think of anti-virus (AV); before you run the infected code, the job of the AV system is to yell "stop" if the code has an infection. Intrusion systems (whether intrusion detection or intrusion prevention) are 100% about this and exactly so. A lot of network perimeter controls, including denial of service handlers, exist to recognize a negative while it is still a small negative, before it has time to grow into a big negative. Synthetic execution ("sandboxing") goes so far as to actually test the what if scenario in a bomb-proof room. This is all part of a wonderful theory and very nearly a wonderful practice. As the aphorism says, an ounce of prevention is worth a pound of cure.

Recognizing a negative is where that ounce of prevention lies, and particularly so in the digital sphere. It is one thing to infiltrate a terrorist into an airport, say, but because of the way digital threats not only move but also clone themselves, once a digital invader is inside the city walls there is no longer any way to say how many invaders there are. The question may as well be both unanswerable and irrelevant. As such, there definitely are places where a digital defense does need to challenge that which would enter, would launch, or would simply pass by, because there are definitely places where if that is not done, there will be no way to recover short of starting over. As someone truly in a position to know said,

> When you are dealing with rootkits and some advanced spyware programs, the only solution is to rebuild from scratch. In some cases, there really is no way to recover without nuking the systems from orbit. [18]

That is what we are up against: recognizing negatives well enough to avoid having to just plain start over. Our problem is the "good enough security" problem: How much of the negative do we have to recognize to make recognizing negatives worth anything?

Recognizing negatives is getting harder and it is getting harder fast. First, the number of vulnerabilities continues to rise. As Figure 16 demonstrates, the number of new vulnerabilities per unit time is still rising despite the much increased effort of all software vendors to stamp out vulnerabilities in their code.

Second, where the vulnerabilities are is increasingly in the applications running on desktops, not on servers or in the core operating systems themselves. Figure 17 recasts NIST data for counts of remotely exploitable

---

[18] Mike Danseglio, Program Manager, Security Solutions Group, Microsoft, April 3, 2006.

[19] "Internet Security Threat Report XII" (07H1), Symantec, September, 2007, at `www.symantec.com/enterprise/threatreport/index.jsp`

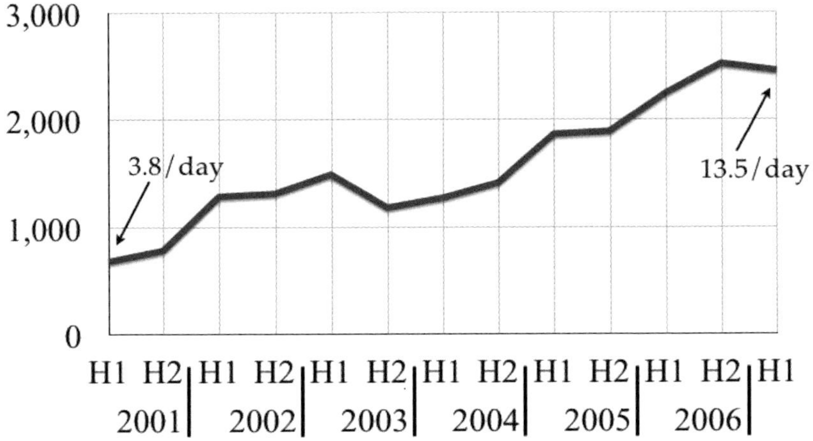

Figure 16: Vulnerabilities reported to/by Symantec[19] per semi-annual intervals

vulnerabilities to vulnerability market share by type. It is pretty obvious that non-server applications are where the flaws are, and thus where the attack risk is.

Third, private communications with each of the top three anti-virus vendors confirms that unless there are at least 50,000 desktops involved, it is not likely that a signature for a new threat will be forthcoming. This is not malfeasance; it is risk management in the face of a deluge of vulnerabilities and the self-mutating malware that exploits them.

---

[20] NIST data, drawn from `icat.nist.gov/icat.cfm?function=statistics`

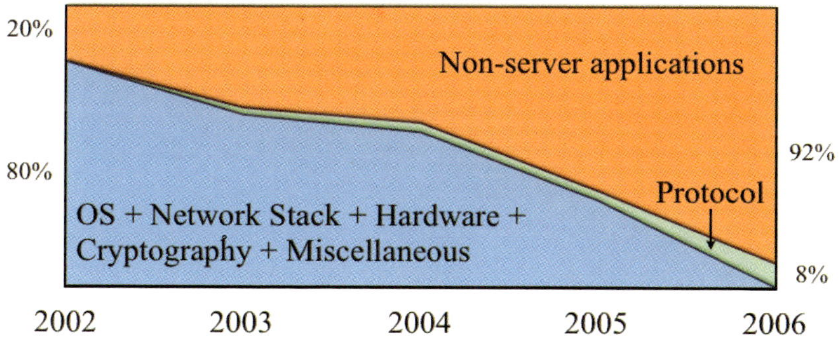

Figure 17: Share of all remotely exploitable vulnerabilities reported to/by NIST[20] per annual intervals

Fourth, malware is rapidly moving toward hiding its presence ("stealth") and leaving no or diversionary tracks ("anti-forensic"). The sum of these four points, a rising tide of vulnerabilities despite best efforts all around, the dominance of non-server applications on the desktop as to where those vulnerabilities are, the general and undeniable defeat of those who produce signatures of malware to keep up with the rate of incoming fire, and the increasing expertness of malware's own risk management, leads to the direct conclusion that recognizing a negative is a rear-guard action now. It cannot keep up, and it will not keep up. Don't drop your shields, but do drop your rose-colored glasses.

While all that is going on, more and more regulations, both public (formal) regulation and private (contractual) regulation, call for the holder of important data to prove a negative. "Prove a negative" in this context means to be able to show to a skeptical party that such and such a thing did not happen. If you lose customer private data, then in many locales you are then obligated to tell those customers that you did, but with the nuance that once a breach has occurred, the operational assumption is that data that cannot be shown to have not been lost must be treated as if it was lost. Put differently, the implicit multiple choice question the regulations ask you may begin like this:

> Did you lose this data item?
> (a) Yes
> (b) No
> (c) Don't know
> (d) Don't understand
> (e) Would rather not answer

is really

> Did you lose this data item?
> (b1) No, and I can prove it
> (a+b0+c+d+e) Anything other than (b1)

Put differently, no one cares unless you can answer No and you can prove it; just answering No is not enough. While this is the simplest explanation, there is a stronger one. At least in the U.S., since December, 2006, the so-called "E-Discovery" changes to the Federal

Rules of Civil Procedure[21] have been in place. What this means to you and to your firm is that if electronic data becomes a matter of interest in a judicial proceeding, then that data will not be admitted into evidence if you cannot respond in prove-a-negative fashion to a challenge to it. You have to prove, not assert, that the data you hold was collected in a way that is consistent with the truth and that you held it in a way that is consistent with its integrity. As they say in Court, "Do you swear that this is the truth, the whole truth, and nothing but the truth, so help you God?" and it applies here.

The implications of this are yet to be felt or understood in the large, but we can already say with some assurance that data security has not only become more important, but more like "prove a negative." Can you show that no one fabricated what you brought in? Can you show that no one preferentially deleted parts of what you brought in? Those two questions alone are scary enough, but without going into it at all, have your General Counsel read the Zubulake decision[22] if he or she hasn't already done so. Judge Scheindlin set several precedents in that case that exactly germane to the idea of the burden being on you to prove a negative.

As it happens, this "prove a negative" does in fact lead somewhere. As a matter of science, to prove that

---

[21] Amendments to the Federal Rules of Civil Procedure, Rule 16, available on-net at `www.uscourts.gov/rules/EDiscovery_w_Notes.pdf`

[22] Zubulake *v* UBS Warburg LLC, 220 F.R.D. 212, 216 (S.D. N.Y. 2003), `www.nysd.uscourts.gov/rulings/02cv01243_072403.pdf`

something did not happen you must have every place where it could happen under surveillance. This may be distasteful, and to the present author surveillance of any sort whatsoever borders on anathema, but as a practical matter in a world hostile to your interests, it will pay you to surveil yourself. The way it will pay you is that it, and it alone, will enable you to say "I can prove that X did not happen because I have records of everything that did happen, and X is not in there." The subtext is that you will then have to defend how it is that you have these records and are they what you say they are, but this sort of proof is the only proof available when proving a negative is the order of the day. Any society that requires this has given up on the presumption of innocence, or, to be charitable, in the electronic sphere there is no presumption of innocence nor can there be given the facts of the electronic world being as they are. "I know that Mr. X was not here because he was there" works in the physical world, but not in the digital world where all copies have 100% fidelity.

If and when you undertake surveillance, you will come to a fork in the road, namely the choice of what is the unit of surveillance you will choose. Is it "one person" or is it "one datum." Might we suggest that if you care for liberty that the unit of casual observation be one datum rather than one person. Yes, the databases that accrue from the one alternative or the other are homomorphic to each other, but when the acts of surveillance are precautionary and preventative, it would be better to have the records thus collected not be in convenient form for looking at all one person does. Besides, if your argument is that of protecting value, it is the data that has the value and thus the data that should be watched, at least until such time that you have probable cause to watch a person.

4.3. Data security as a tax *vs.* as an investment

Security has long been thought of as purely a cost center item. It gets in the way, it creates friction in the same sense that an economist means friction — it distorts the relationship between two parties to a communication, to a transaction, or to a task. The gold standard for any security scheme has always come down to two single words: no-load and inescapable. The inescapable part is perhaps obvious; a security scheme that can be circumvented isn't a security scheme. The no-load part is the minimization of the operational tax that security can impose. If you need six layers of badges and a necklace of USB tokens to get your work done, then security is a tax. All border control, physical and/or electronic, is just such a tax. In digital security as in society, the best aim is no new taxes.

So if we are first going to look at data security as a tax, which is to say as a cost-side question, then we are clearly looking to balance costs. Nevertheless, while all taxes may be theft, we have to pay some inside-the-company taxes if we are to get digital security — another tradeoff between, in this case, the cost of protection, which is the tax you elect to pay in the absence of an event, and the cost of cleaning up failures that may occur if you do not elect to pay the tax. We treat that in the chapter entitled "Economic Parsimony,"

Note however that when discussing how much to spend on data security, part of the consideration will be "How much is everyone else spending?" We are outside the realm of technical considerations when we ask that, but if you are an outlier in that distribution then someone will ask why you are. If you are spending much below, then the occurrence of an unhappy data security event will probably end up exposing that you are well off the standard tax (cost) that other firms pay. If you are spending much above, then you better have a good reason since your own management committee or your auditors will have something to say about that in due course. Probably everyone reading this book will have had a conversation like this one:

CFO: How much did we spend on data security last year?
You: $10,000,000 not counting compliance.
CFO: And how many security events did we have?
You: I'm proud to say "none."
CFO: Then we spent too much money.

This is actually far from silly. In this business, if you truly say and truly believe something like "Failure is not an option," then you are going to have to overspend because you are going to have to make failure an outlier. This is where data security parts company with quality control. Yes, "failure is not an option" is what so-called Six Sigma programs are all about, but the issue in data security is that our failure modes are not the random bad luck of physical breakage or discoordination between parts of the enterprise. Our opponents are sentient, and that — sentient opponents — makes all the difference. It is even what makes a security product a security product.

If a product does not have sentient opponents, then it is not a security product. This is best examined by looking at why products fail — if the reasons that a product fails is some collection of clueless users ("Hey, watch this!"), alpha particles, or discharged batteries, then it is not a security product. Bruce Schneier, in his Foreword to Ross Anderson's Security Engineering, put it best:

> Security involves making sure things work, not in the presence of random faults, but in the face of an intelligent and malicious adversary trying to ensure that things fail in the worst possible way at the worst possible time... again and again.[23]

If the reason a product fails is because some gleeful clown discovers that he can be the superuser by typing 5,000 lower-case "A"s into some prompt, then said clown may not be all that sentient but nevertheless we are talking about a security product. It is not stray neutrons but rather sentient opponents that makes all the difference.

This is why it is often better to look at data security not as a tax but as an investment. Nobody thinks of an

---

[23] Anderson R, Security Engineering, HERE, 19 HERE.

investment and imagines perfection; no, they imagine (hope) that for a certain outlay there will be a corresponding return. Investment is a risk management practice that taxation never is; it trades one downside for another, and it is about odds. In its simplest form, it doesn't even require absolute scale.

Take for example something as simple as whether to install a patch or not. You make an investment decision when you do or do not install that patch. You can even measure it. Run your application scanner against the code that has a patch waiting. Take the resulting vulnerability score, r_a, as a risk index. Apply the patch, and run your scanner again to get a second risk index, r_b. Look up the cost of rolling out a patch, c_r. Your decision to invest or not is whether the reduction in risk is worth the price, i.e., whether

$$\frac{r_a - r_b}{c_r} \geq threshold$$

This does assume that you can set a threshold, but that is precisely what we mean by making failure an option: You have to know when it is worth playing the game and when it is not, what a poker player might describe as "Know when to hold 'em and know when to fold 'em."

If you are risk tolerant, then your thresholds will be high. If you are risk averse, then your thresholds will be low. You almost surely have different thresholds for different settings. For data that is truly catastrophic to lose, the threshold will be low. An example of that might be the formulas for new pharmaceutical compounds in that critical interval between when some researcher in some lab yells "Eureka!" and you when you get your new drug patent filing in. Other data may not be all that terrible to lose; your copy of the NYSE ticker from a week ago is easy to get refreshed should you lose the one you have. Risk aversion is not bad nor is risk tolerance bad. You can be averse to risks you know just as you can be averse to risks you don't know. This, too, can be assessed. Let's illustrate... The circle is a fair coin toss (probability is 0.5 to either branch) and the payoff is either you win $\$R$ or you lose $\$R/2$. Your expected return for playing is

$$(.5 \times R) + (.5 \times \frac{-R}{2}) = \frac{R}{4}$$

Now, how big an R will you play for? That is your risk

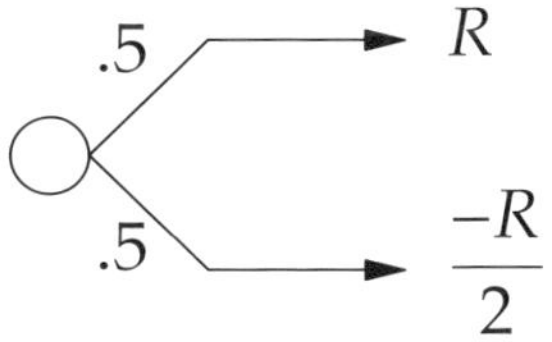

Figure 18: Differential payoff to measure risk tolerance[24]

[24] Raiffa H: Decision Analysis, Addison-Wesley, 1968.

tolerance, at least for this game. While the game is about *you*, you can also see how this could translate into uneven probabilities and the value of something else, like your data.

Let's go a step further, and in Figure 0 look at risk aversion versus risk seeking. The game here is a fair coin toss where you have a 50% chance of winning $100 with no downside. Your expected value is $50. Now someone else offers you $G to take your place in this game. The question is, what $G would you accept? How much certain gain will you trade for an uncertain outcome?

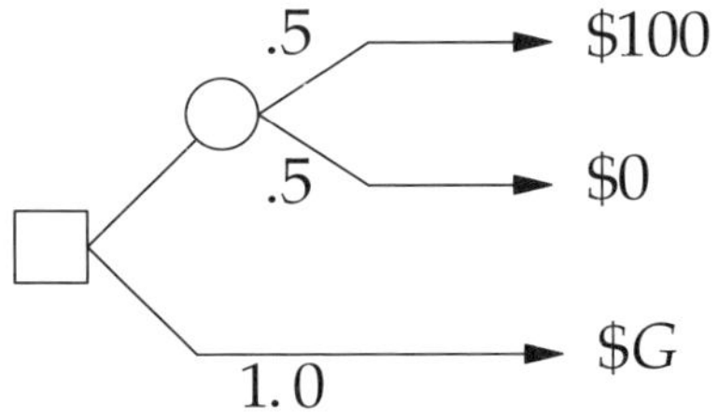

Figure 19: Choice vs. chance to measure risk aversion[25]

---

[25] *ibid.*

$G<50$ means you are risk averse
$G=50$ means you are risk neutral
$G>50$ means you are risk loving

Whatever $\$G$ you accept, $\$50-\$G$ is your "risk premium."

Now all this may seem silly, but it (again) is not. Risk aversion is, for example, why we buy insurance. To stay in business, the insurance firm must be overcharging you for the actual value of your risk and you must be buying that insurance because you are risk averse. All well and good. When facing choices with comparable returns, agents tend to chose the less-risky alternative.[26] More to the point, we are risk averse in proportion to our ignorance. That we are risk averse means we tax ourselves rather than invest in ourselves. Simply put, we need to be less ignorant so that we can be less risk averse. With data security, we have to know more about what data we have to know more about how it moves or we will have to be risk averse.

4.4. Winning asymmetric wars *vs.* diverting attack to others

The war we are in, and it *is* a war, is over retaining control of our data. The problem is, that war is asymmetric. Our costs of defense are greater than, and rise

---

[26] A direct quote from Friedman M & Savage LP: "The Utility Analysis of Choices Involving Risk," Journal of Political Economy, v56 pp279-304, 1948.

faster than, the costs of offense from our opponents. Or, to be precise, nearly all the conventional mechanisms of defense put the defender at an asymmetric disadvantage. Consider Figure 20: which is the number of never before seen data-theft malware found in phishing e-mail per month. In other words, in December, 2006, say, reports of 345 never-before-seen varieties of data-theft malware were received, and in January, 2007, reports of another 340 never-before-seen varieties were received. This is a chart of "incidence," in other words. Those incidence figures are interesting enough, but the real

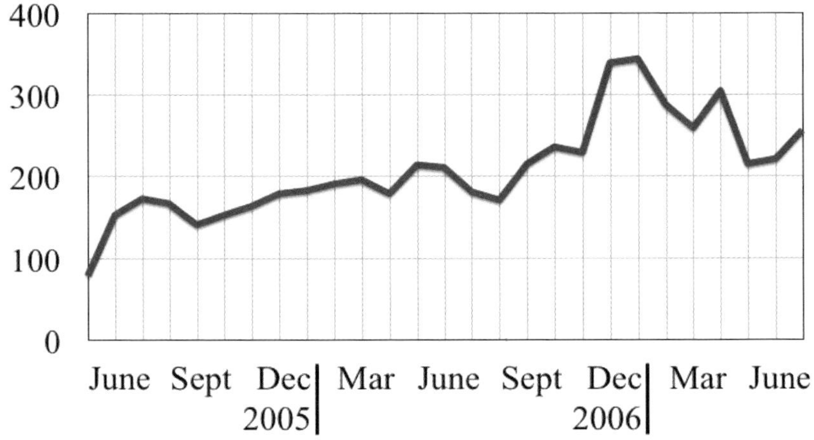

Figure 20: New data-theft malware in phishing e-mail per month[27]

[27] Data from the Anti-Phishing Working Group (APWG) as released monthly; see antiphishing.org/reports/apwg_report_july_2007.pdf

point is in Figure 21: which illustrates the asymmetry. You, as defender, have to be able to recognize and block any data-theft malware in circulation. Your workfactor, as defender, is thus the sum of all the data-theft malware the opponents have invented. This means your workfactor for data-theft-malware in phishing e-mails alone has a 710% compound annual growth rate (CAGR). The opponent's workfactor does *not* grow at this rate; the opponent's workfactor is proportional not to the cumulative sum of all data-theft malware that has come before but rather to the workfactor cost of creating new data-theft malware that you (the defender) have not yet seen. Since the opponent has largely automated this process, you are now in an asymmetric warfare

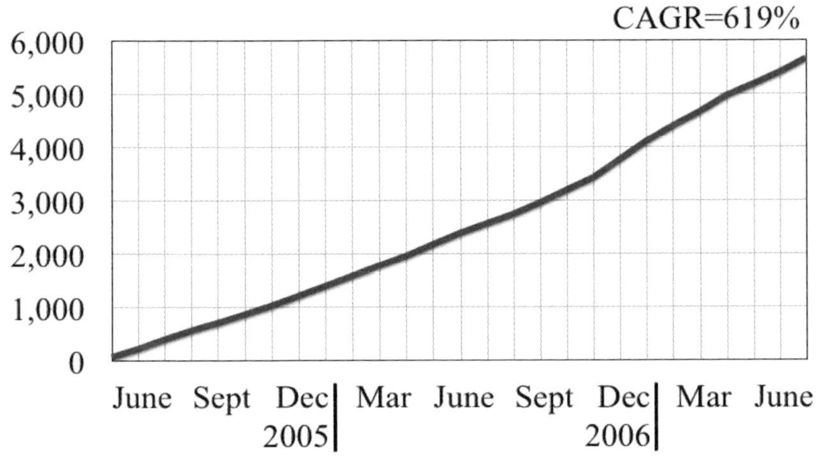

Figure 21: Cumulative new data-theft malware in phishing e-mail per month

situation. Their workfactor is largely constant and certainly small. Yours has a CAGR of 619%. That's the point.

In such an asymmetric situation, it is only a matter of time before the opponent has the upper hand. Frankly, they already do. To address this asymmetry one of two things must be possible. The one alternative is for you to continue to endure and simply meet the cost of so enduring. In some circumstances in life, to bear any burden is entirely warranted. Winston Churchill's speeches were replete with this idea.[28] For occasions not as stern, the advice is just as direct, and we will deal with it presently:

If you are losing a game you cannot afford to lose,
then you must change the rules.

[28] "Never give in. Never give in. Never, never, never, never — in nothing, great or small, large or petty — never give in, except to convictions of honor and good sense. Never yield to force. Never yield to the apparently overwhelming might of the enemy." October 29, 1941, at Harrow School.

5. Economics and economic parsimony

We've all heard of "a solution looking for a problem" and we've all had interviews with salesmen hawking cool things that were more cool than valuable. We've all read about this or that boondoggle where good money followed bad and delivery dates receded with each new infusion of cash. We've all had our own experiences with products where what it does and what it was said to do didn't match for long. In most if not all of these cases the outcome can be traced back to solving the wrong problem. Sometimes this is bad luck, sometimes ignorance, sometimes mission creep, sometimes chutzpah, sometimes egotism. Regardless of why, the effect is the same: some problem gets solved but it is not the problem that matters. How do we avoid this?

With data security to get the problem statement right is hard: We are not starting from scratch, there is a lot of infrastructure already in place, some things are untouchable, some of the most important decisions have had very subtle arguments behind them but the logic has been lost. To understand where in security we are we have to know how we got here. Otherwise, momentum alone will otherwise carry us through further decisions whether we mean for it to or not. For those wondering where this chapter is leading here's the punchline: A lot of security technologies deserve no further investment.

For "security" to add value it must offer calibrated economic tradeoffs between rational valuation of information and differential costs of its protection. It has to make sense economically — or it will not last. We thus define our problem as the maximum data protection at the minimum cost, the "minimax" solution; "optimizing spend," if you prefer. This can be more security for the same price, less price for the same security, or something in between. Economic facts of life, in other words, like anywhere else.

5.1. How to see

There are two analytic paths to a minimax solution: cost-benefit and cost-effectiveness. "Cost-benefit analysis" (CBA) compares costs and benefits with the idea of getting the maximum benefit for the minimum cost, consistent with a minimax viewpoint. To work where there are multiple alternatives, cost-benefit analysis requires that costs and benefits be calibrated to a common currency. It doesn't matter what currency, so long as it puts all the alternatives on a common scale. CBA attempts to answer "Should we spend the money?"

Cost-benefit questions, however, can be hard to answer. For example, how many US dollars is a human life worth? Would you rather have an afternoon to yourself or an hundred gallons of gas? Would you rather have cheap timber or wilderness? Is a blemish-free record proof that you are spending too much on security?

In cost-benefit analysis, the first job is convert apples to oranges; once done, the outcome of CBA is then maximization of total value. Formulaically, CBA looks for the best value of this equation

$$CBratio = \frac{cost_{new\ strategy}}{benefit_{new\ strategy}}$$

which is a favorable ratio only when it is less than unity (< 1). Decision making will eventually compare $CBratio_i$ with $CBratio_j$ and so forth, and all the benefits must be in the same units as the costs.

By contrast, "cost-effectiveness analysis" (CEA) first fixes the cost and then seeks what you can get for that cost. Instead of "Would you spend $1M for five more years of life?" cost-effectiveness asks "You are going to spend that $1M one way or another; would you rather have ten more years of life at half your current energy level or five years at full steam?" Would you rather your relatives visited twice for one week or once for two weeks? Are more lives saved by spending $100M on safer cars or by spending $100M on traffic law enforcement? In the electrical system, is it better to work on mean-time-between-failure or on mean-time-to-repair?"

Cost-effectiveness analysis measures marginal value, the incremental expansion of an outcome compared to an incremental expansion of a cost of acquiring that outcome. Formulaically, it looks like this:

$$CE\ ratio = \frac{cost_{new\ strategy} - cost_{current\ practice}}{effect_{new\ strategy} - effect_{current\ practice}}$$

which is also a favorable ratio when it is less than unity (< 1). CEA attempts to answer "What can we get for the money?"

Perhaps it is thus obvious that CEA is more likely to be tractable everywhere while CBA is tractable only for those cases where the conversion of value to a common currency can be realistically expected to converge. Because CEA does not depend on settling matters of taste (like "How much is a human life worth?"), CEA is much akin to looking at trend data whereas CBA is more like looking at raw measurements.

So what does a commitment to CEA get us in the case of data security? The more open the corporation's business model the more data matters and hence the more data security matters. In turn, the more data security matters the more it is essential to acknowledge the insider threat. This shifts what minimax problem it is that optimal security is positioned to solve, what an effective solution looks like, and what it costs. In a corporate setting such as yours, it is especially valuable when a budget is more like a block grant and less like a list of earmarked projects.

Information security costs are of two kinds: anticipation costs and failure costs. "Anticipation costs" are the monies you spend to avoid problems. "Failure costs" are the monies you spend for repair and/or recourse. Zero spend on anticipation maximizes spend on remediation while near-infinite spend on anticipation zeroes out failure costs. Any given strategy will be a mix of voluntary spending on anticipation plus involuntary spending on failure. The total cost of security will thus be the sum of the cost curves for anticipation and for failure. A minimax solution for security spend will be the low point of this combined curve.

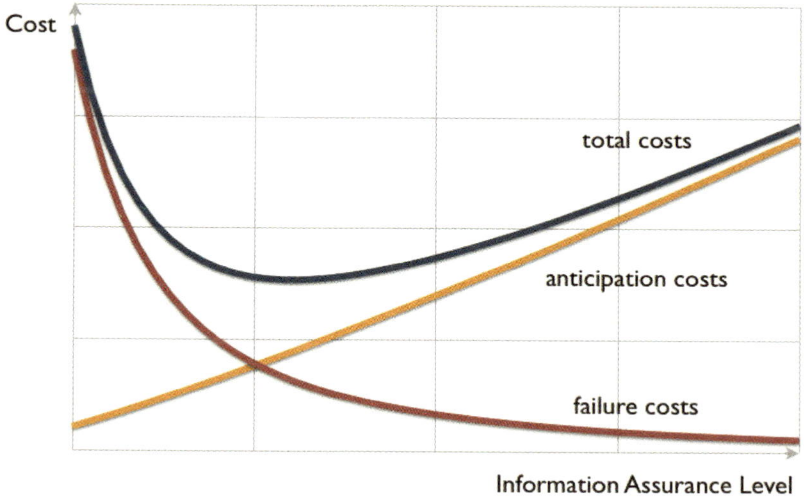

Figure 22: crossing curves and the minimax idea

As Figure 22 demonstrates, the minimax solution is where the sum of the cost curve of anticipation plus the cost curve of failure is the least. In the sample figure, it is just to the right of where the two curves cross.

Your curves for anticipation and for failure, and thus the minimax solution point, are themselves subject to other forces, particularly the degree of of electronic collaboration and coordination you have with your customers, suppliers, and trading partners. If you have little collaboration, then failure costs will be small and thus anticipation costs will drive optimal spend. If your collaboration is massive, failure costs will be likewise massive and so failure costs, not anticipation costs, will drive the optimal spend. In Figure 23, three graphs show this progression:

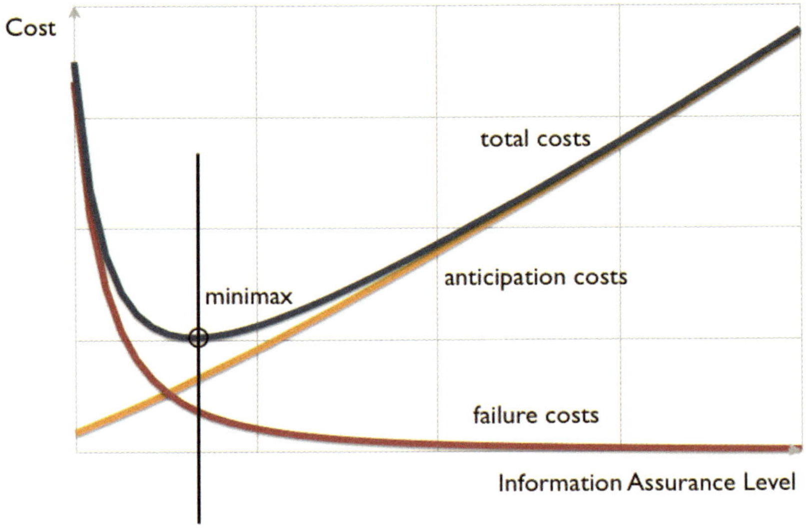

Figure 23a: low collaboration

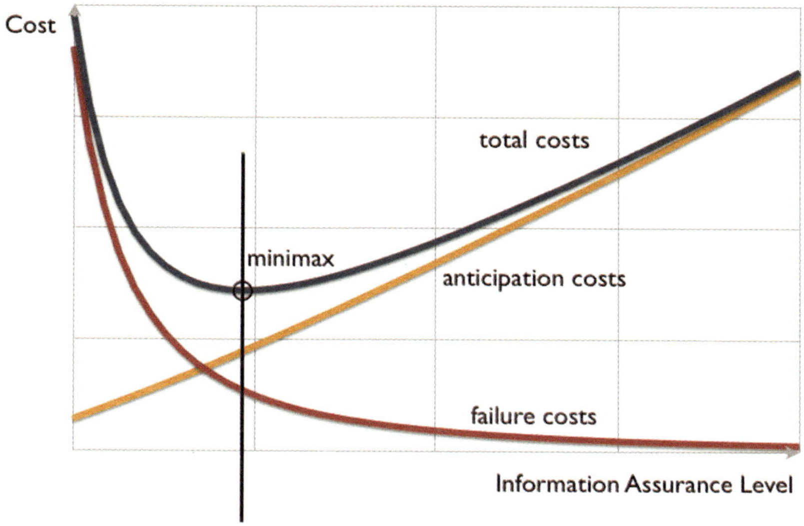

Figure 23b: middling collaboration

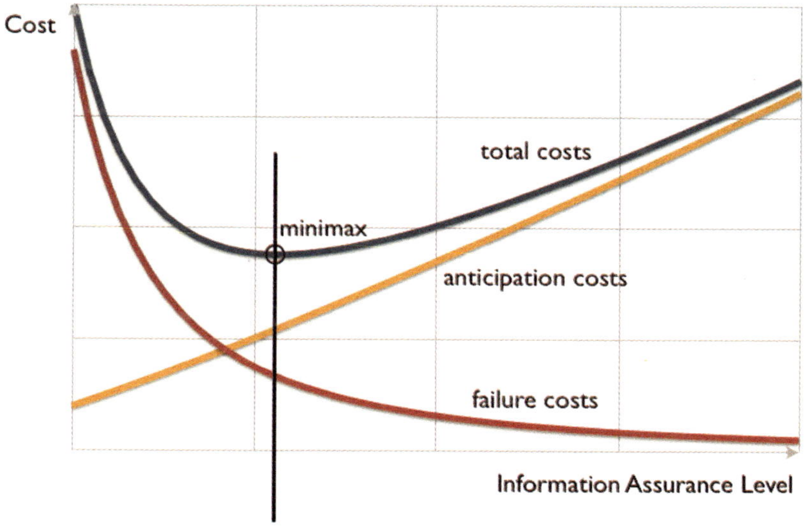

Figure 23c: high collaboration

As you can see, as collaboration increases the optimal spend increases, but the minimax solution will still be found where the summation curve bottoms out. It will be the job of a CEA to understand the summed curve, but let's first look at where these costs come from.

5.2. Where anticipation costs come from

Anticipation costs mount upward in reaction to a steady stream of new risks and, to a lesser extent, increasing virulence of existing risks. When each then-new class of risk arose, someone thought up a new class of product to deal with that risk. That past predicts our future though, of course, a new class of risk is not a daily occurrence even though it has happened more than once in the work lifetime of everyone reading this note. It is thus instructive to understand the anticipation costs contributed by the most common products protecting against the most common classes of threats. First, a definition...

> Total Cost of Ownership (TCO)
> The all encompassing set of costs — everything from capital to license fees to service costs to budgeted as well as unbudgeted labor costs.

Any all-inclusive discussion needs to embrace the TCO concept, but we do not need a specific methodology for computing a TCO, just the acknowledgment that one exists and that it is multifaceted. Those facets include:

- For any control system in the real world, exception handling is more expensive than routine management. Under the downward price pressure of automation, the spread between the cost of exception handling and the cost of automated, routine management broadens over time. Exception handling costs therefore deserve the greatest management focus as their relative share of TCO rises as other shares fall.
- The urgency of security grows as the product of the value being protected times the magnitude of the threat. If both the value and the threat are growing, the urgency of security grows especially quickly.
- The minimal product mix barely covers all requirements, thereby limiting capitalization and routine maintenance costs. If there were no exception handling then we would be done now.
- Where there is exception handling, the best situation is where the exception handling of any one product is preempted by the routine processing of another. A different topic than today, but this is generally known as defense-in-depth.

To really nail down our minimax solution we will need to (1) calculate a cost for defense and (2) put a value on our information. We look first at the TCO for the typical melange of security products and then at valuing information.

5.3. Technologies that have peaked

Existing desktop agents are commodities and their TCO is dominated by exception handling. They do not counter-protect each other, thus when those products fail there is non-zero residual risk. The four main desktop mechanisms for protecting information at point of use: Antivirus (AV), Firewalls (FW), Intrusion Detection Systems (IDS), and Patch Management (PM).

5.3.1. Antivirus

The problem statement for antivirus: *Recognize malware at minimum latency and minimum load.* This is hard, it will get harder, and at the limit it is impossible. This is bad news if the risk is growing, and it is. The warning interval before pervasive exposure of desktops to infection is shortening. Virus payloads are growing more complex and harder to eradicate. Constant mutation of virus code ("polymorphism") is becoming more prevalent, and all these points are summed up[29] in Figure 24, which verifies that polymorphism is accelerating.

The need for prompt delivery of new signature rules assures that only a push-model to existing subscribers will be able to keep up with the quickening pace of attacks. TCO is dominated by the exception handling of firedrills and the compliance review of

[29] *op cit.*, Symantec ISTR:xii

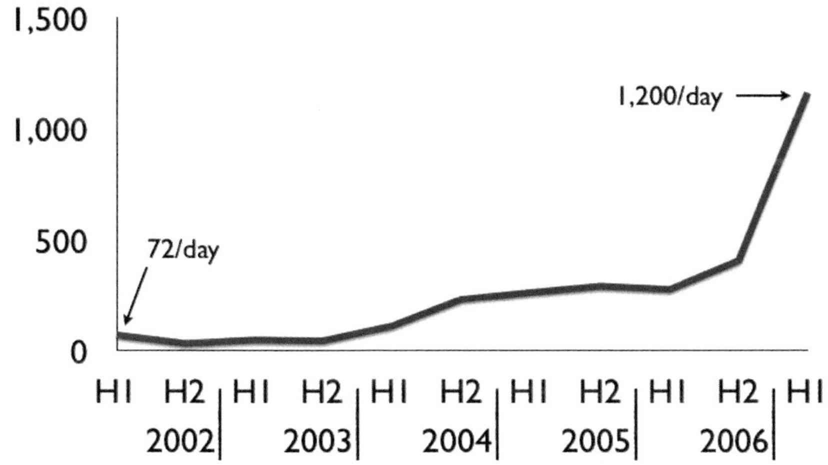

Figure 24: New malware detected per day

consistency, desktop to desktop. All definitions carry with them a possibility of disabling legitimate code, so the risk tradeoff is between the risk of unrecognized infection and the risk of unintended consequents. For those who value reliability above all else, this means a fire drill when there is an untested virus signature file to install. And when antivirus fails, the effects of an attack may be hard to reverse as those effects may be intentionally well hidden.

5.3.2. Firewall

The problem statement for the firewall is parallel to that of antivirus: *Intervene in the process of network packet delivery so as to recognize malware and to do so at minimum latency and minimum load.* The inspection needs to be made in near real time. At the end of the road, this, too, is impossible as an encrypted stream, once established, is uninspectable. More generally, knowing that this or that content is bad is an even harder problem than the antivirus problem. (Computer scientists would say it is provably impossible to truly say whether any code is good or bad.)

TCO is dominated by change management and the cost of maintaining coherence across firewall fleets. Coherence is itself hard enough that secondary commercial products exist for this purpose alone. When the firewall fails any entity for which the firewall was the sole means of defense is then open to compromise. The risk of that compromise depends then on two characteristics, the duration of the failure (and associated duration of exposure) and the defenselessness of what the firewall protected.

5.3.3. IDS

The problem statement for the intrusion detection system is to: *Correlate sniffed network evidence to detect attacks in progress.* Host-based IDSs look simultaneously at logs, data, network streams, *etc.* Some are signature-based and some focus on anomaly detection. Anomaly detection requires a mechanism for defining an anomaly at wire speed thus, in turn, IDS systems require either hand tuning or an operational tolerance for high-levels of false positive reports. Operating at wire speeds is difficult when traffic volumes are robust but even when traffic is low a patient attacker will be able to fly below the IDS radar as it were.

There is substantial overlap in the functionality of a firewall and an intrusion detection system. TCO is dominated by change management (keeping current) plus the cost of investigating false positives versus the cost of not intervening in what turn out to be false negatives. When an IDS fails, presumably an attacker gets through. What happens after that depends, of course, on what's left to defend and with what is that defense mounted.

5.3.4. Patch Management

The problem statement for patch management is to *Ensure that the files that are on the machine are the right files.* PM workfactor is dominated by peak-loads as when a patch is available everyone presumably needs to get it. In an effort to slow reverse-engineering of patches for exploits, major vendors such as Microsoft now bundle their patches together which maximizes the peak-load problem. PM functionally provides inventory and replacement of files at a distance. It is commoditized to a greater degree than any of AV, FW or IDS, often to the point of being an operating system feature, *per se.* Besides trading off the risk of breaking that which is presently running with the risk of being broken by exploits, PM carries a substantial if unlikely risk that were the patch management system itself to be taken over by hostile parties the game would be entirely over. As such it is perhaps the exemplar of a tradeoff between a small risk of a large loss and a large risk of a small loss. When PM fails the usual impact is to break an existing application, which might be said to thus simulate an effective attack on that application by an outsider, however inadvertent that "attack" might be.

5.4. You get what you pay for, but not forever

Each of those four main technologies does what it does but even with a limited view of what security means the challenges are tough. There is continual requirements creep and there is an ever more challenging operational setting.[30] TCO for each of the four is overwhelmingly dominated by the costs of management and not the initial purchase of software licenses (quantity-one retail price of all four combined is less than $150). TCO intangibles like testing, downtime, tracking, spare capacity for firedrills, *etc.*, make these "security" products an increasing fraction of the total

> Malware production continue to rise and to do so at increasing rates, such that they no mimic diseases of the immune system. IDS and Firewall vendors are duplicating each other's functionality to the point that the marginal benefit of the one added to the other is falling. The time to reverse engineer patches and build exploits has, through automation, fallen to the level of a few hours thus truly making a patch an advertisement for the vulnerability it addresses.

TCO for the desktop.[30]

In all of AV, FW, IDS, and/or PM, you do get no data for management beyond counting the number of alarms, or the number of patches to be pushed down, or a list of potential intrusions that have to then be investigationally proven to be false positives. In other words, each of those systems does an incomplete job and what news it brings you is bad news while, with the exception of PM, none help you fix anything. Each may be perfect at what it does, but the failure of any is the failure of all.

5.5. Where failure costs come from

Failure costs in information protection are proportional to information value, *per se*. These costs are some combination of the aftermath from a loss of data integrity (unauthorized data modification), a loss of data confidentiality (unauthorized data exposure), and a loss data availability (unauthorized blocking of access to data). These costs are thus both a function of time (how long before you detect and/or how long before you repair, assuming that you can repair) and a function of value.

---

[30] An academic environment, like the University of Washington, estimates \$3K/year/desktop while Fortune and The Economist estimate \$4-8K/year/desktop. Security at \$1000+/year/desktop out of a total \$4-8K/year/desktop is a meaningful number at enterprise scale, enough so that some financial institutions are effectively returning to a time-share model.

While everyone agrees that information is valuable, that is generally as far as agreement goes. In the study of statistics, a difficulty in figuring the value of "X" may sometimes be avoided by figuring the value of "1 – X" which is to say that solving a problem may involve changing your point of view to one where the problem is tractable yet the solution equivalent. For example, "How much is your brand worth?" won't get a consensus answer in any Board room, but re-abstracting the question to "Starting from scratch, what's the minimum money and time it would take to build a brand as good as the one you have now?" might get you a consensus lower bound just from changing the point of view. If that lower bound is sufficiently large to make a security decision easy, then you are both using reputation value as a numerical quantity yet not getting hung up on precision.

> At a New York trading bank, the CISO had an analysis which showed that such and such a security investment was cost effective if the reputation of the bank was worth at least one basis point (0.01%) of the market capitalization. Since no budget officer would opine that the reputation of the bank was worth less than a basis point of market cap, the project was speedily approved. A true story of clever inside marketing.

So even if we cannot measure the value of information we can ask what costs we would incur if we did not have the information (or if someone else did). We can ask how much equally trustable replacement information would cost us, starting from where we are and knowing what we now know. We can ask what is the price of delay while recovery happens and thus choose between investment for making failure less likely and and investment for making recovery more timely.

A fool can ask questions that a wise man cannot answer, and in that sense "What's your information worth?" isn't likely to help. However, just because we cannot name a figure at four digit accuracy all is far from lost. Take a look at the decision you have to make and see if that decision actually requires a precise valuation — odds are that it does not, rather it requires that an inequality ("If it is more valuable than X then the right course of action is...") The boxed vignette thus illustrates two information value points: Reputation is a correlate of security and that an inequality is good enough for decision making.

5.6. A unifying abstraction

We discussed anticipation costs first because that is what everyone is already doing. We discussed failure costs where it is more talk and less numbers and where the specifics of the individual firm matter more. We now discuss a way to pull these two together, to find the minimax point where the sum of the anticipation costs and the failure costs bottoms out and the ratio of security achieved to cost expended is maximum.

The more open the corporation's business model the more information security contracts to the point of use and value, *i.e.*, the data object. The conventional approach to protecting information is access control and, if threat and value are rising, this means access control at ever finer grain. But access control as a security technology suffers from complexity issues related to scale. Consider the generalized access control problem, perhaps best illustrated as the matrix shown in Figure 25. In such a matrix you have the possible requestors of access to a resource, denoted here by A, B, C, *etc.*, and the resources to which the requestors might seek access, denoted here by 1, 2, 3, *etc.* The access control problem is thus the problem of accurately maintaining the right

resources

people	1	2	3	4	5	6	7	8	9	10	11	12	13	14	...
A	√														
B							√			√	√		√	√	
C	√		√	√	√	√			√					√	
D			√			√	√			√	√	√		√	
E		√	√	√	√			√		√		√	√	√	
...															

Figure 25: The access control problem in matrix representation

check marks in the right boxes in this matrix. As such, if there is any finite lower bound in the cost of maintaining a single check-mark in this matrix, then the overall cost of maintaining the matrix as a whole grows as the product of the number of entities that can initiate a request and the number of entities that can be the object of such a request. In other words, it is geometric, not linear, in the size of the organization: a doubling of an organization's size is likely to double both its personnel and its resources thus increasing the size of this matrix by a factor of four. In exactly the same way, increasing the precision of access control grows costs: going from "require password at login" to "assign all employees to roles and all roles to program sets" is an increase in the size of the access control matrix. Any cost that rises faster than linear with growth of the organization is unsustainable over time. Any cost that rises faster than the complexity of environment is unsustainable over time. The CEA view of an organizational doubling under a straight access control model is highly unattractive:

$$CE\ ratio = \frac{cost_{access\ control\ tomorrow} - cost_{access\ control\ today}}{effect_{access\ control\ tomorrow} - effect_{access\ control\ today}}$$

which for the simple case of doubling the organization cost (X) is four times as high but with same effect (Y) as today,

$$CE_{access\ control} = \frac{4X\ cost - 1X\ cost}{2Y\ effect - 1Y\ effect} = 3$$

With accountability as your model, your unit of cost is

not the matrix of what might happen but the events that do happen, which are linear with the size of the enterprise, doubling if the enterprise doubles.

$$CE_{accountability} = \frac{2X\ cost - 1X\ cost}{2Y\ effect - 1Y\ effect} = 1$$

and the ratio is considerably more favorable than for growing the access control matrix. Had we used CBA instead, we would now be comparing whether an access control model is more to our taste than an accountability model, and whether we would want to spend the money at all. If your organization is growing or if your organization wants to be finer grained about what its security system oversees, then you are going to spend money. As many security budgets are set as a fixed percentage of the overall IT budget, you may already be doing CEA without having realized it.

But back to the point: The economics of the access-control model of information security simply do not scale; economics favor an accountability model focused on the monitoring of information use rather than the gatekeeping of information access. Not only does access control not scale, but, which is worse, it both does not reach files already on the desktop while being perpetually at risk of getting in the way of real work. Access control is thus not a preferred alternative going forward though throwing away existing access control systems is not our target either; it just time to slow or stop further investment in access control and its four bodyguards.

In summary, the abstraction that is now called for is as follows: Security that gets in the way is security that is circumvented, but an accountability system lets things go forward that must go forward. Forensic reconstruction of an electronic accident/crime scene is expensive in proportion to the skill or authority of the attacker, so an accountability model must keep its own records and collect them proactively, not reconstruct them reactively. Some kinds of losses, especially public disclosure of private information, are essentially irreversible, so accountability has to be put into place at the leaf nodes of a network and it has to operate in real time. As nothing is perfect, any accountability system must be itself held accountable.

Whatever system you pick,
this is what it has to do.
This is how to think of the economics,
at least if you still have the freedom to think.

6. Interplay with security metrics

We start this chapter by making clear that the issue of measurement is core to any situation where you are serious about dealing with the unknown. Data security is either about the unknown or it is not, and the only way to convert from divination to mastery is to measure. In this field and at this time, we have gone as far as we can go with adjectives. To go any farther, we have to have numbers. Listen to the wisdom of giants:

> When you can measure what you are speaking about, and express it in numbers, you know something about it; but when you cannot measure it, when you cannot express it in numbers, your knowledge is a meagre and unsatisfactory kind; it may be the beginning of knowledge, but you have scarcely, in your thoughts, advanced to the stage of science.
>
> — William Thomson, Lord Kelvin, 1883

> To measure is to know.
>
> — James Clerk Maxwell, 1831-1879

> Measurement motivates.
>
> — John Kenneth Galbraith

> The revolutionary idea that defines the boundary between modern times and the past is the mastery of risk: the notion that the future is more than a whim of the gods and that men and women are not passive before nature. Until human beings discovered a way across that boundary, the future was the mirror of the

> past or the murky domain of oracles and soothsayers who held a monopoly over knowledge of anticipated events.
>
> — Peter Bernstein, *Against the Gods*, 1996

> The purpose of risk management is to improve the future, not to explain the past. Risk management means taking deliberate action to shift the odds in your favor — increasing the odds of good outcomes and reducing the odds of bad outcomes.
>
> — Dan Borge, *The Book of Risk*, 2001

> Reports that say that something hasn't happened are always interesting to me, because as we know, there are known knowns; there are things we know we know. We also know there are known unknowns; that is to say we know there are some things we do not know. But there are also unknown unknowns; the ones we don't know we don't know.
>
> — Donald Rumsfeld, DoD, 2002

The reason for beginning with these quotations is to make clear why we cannot, repeat can not, speak of data security without speaking of measurement. We've already done this in previous chapters without calling much attention to it as measurement, *per se*. We have, in those cases, used other people's numbers to talk about what situation we find ourselves in with respect to data security.

It is time to come clean about the present author's biases. I am the son of an accountant and trained as a statistician, and I cannot imagine doing information security without numbers. Let me give you some statistical advice: All measurement has bias; the question is whether you can correct for it. My biases pervade my study of data security, but the biggest one is that we have to do what this chapter is about, and that is to get down to some serious metrics.

Not just any metrics. While I do recommend that you get going and measure something, the way I read the sum of those quotes is this: Security metrics are the servants of risk management and risk management is about making decisions, therefore the only security metrics we are interested in are those that support decision making about risk for the purpose of managing that risk. That is what this chapter is about and, with biases flying, why you have no hope of managing your data security risk if you don't include a program of measurement, a program that is about knowing but that is also aware that it is the unknown unknowns that will get you, a program that is directed at the future, not the past, a program that makes motivation possible, a program that makes your future something other than the whim of unseen forces. That is why we are here.

6.1. What can be measured

Generally speaking, the security world's measurements are either counted data ("How many patches are waiting to go out?"), or derivatives of counted data like rates ("How many new patches this week?"), or proportions ("What fraction of machines are 90 days out of patch compliance?"). Not many are directly continuous the way "How tall are you?" is measured on a continuous scale. This will slightly color how we turn measurements into metrics.

The state of the art in security measurement, including data security measurement, is not very good. It's early, what we are measuring is wiggly, and a certain amount of what we are trying to measure has no known baseline. But remember, the purpose of any security measurement is to make decisions, decisions that manage risk. The measurements are thus decision support. They don't explain the past, they make it possible to think about the future and, with some work, to bend that future to your advantage.

For completeness (and to jog the memory of those of you who already know this), there are four kinds of number scales. Nominal scale is simply a list, like "fish" and "bicycle." Ordinal scale is an ordered list, like "$A > B$" and "$B > C$" so, therefore, "$A > C$." Interval scale is a number line where "$2+1=3$" and "$3+1=4$" but which does not have a natural zero, like Celsius temperature. Ratio scale is a number line where there is a natural zero, and where "$2*2=4$" and "$4*2=8$," like Kelvin temperature.

Those distinctions would be irrelevant except for one thing: the minimum you need to make decisions is ordinal scale, to know that one thing is better than another. As it happens, this leads directly to the first bit of advice about measuring anything: Measure it consistently but don't believe the values until much later.

Unless you sure that what you are measuring is both some sort of bedrock and not measured in error, you have to assume that there is error, perhaps both in the offset from wherever "zero" might be and that you are only getting a subset of all the things that are really going on. Take spam e-mail: You cannot tell how much there is because everyone filters hence there is no unmodified stream where you can stand and count "total spam is _____."

What this means is that your focus will be on trends. Trends have ordinal qualities, hence they are generally good enough for decision making ("If A>B, Then GO"). Further, if you really do measure your variable the same way each time, then your tendency to make consistent errors (like catching only some reasonably constant percentage of all outbound e-mail containing credit card numbers) doesn't change the shape of the trendline. Put differently, a street cop never knows, and doesn't need to know, how much heroin is for sale, but he can and must know the price. If that price is falling, then he is losing. If that price is rising, then he is winning. If the rate of change is accelerating, then he knows even more, but he doesn't know the core fact — how much heroin is for sale. Your situation with data security is exactly like that, so your job is to make decisions based on the trends of what you can measure. When you are lucky, you can correlate energy in to effect out.

One additional bit of advice. If you do find a better way to measure something, put that better way into action but don't stop using your old way. You can stop eventually, of course, but if you run both side-by-side for a while then you can calibrate the one against the other and keep your trendline going. The worst thing you can do is to drop the old one and only do the new one. If you do that, you kill your trendline and in addition you kill your ability to infer anything that might be based on that trendline. Just to illustrate, consider Figure 26. This is the number of hosts on the Internet as measured (estimated) by the Internet Systems Consortium. The curve is smooth, but the important thing is that from January, 1995, through July, 1997, they ran two different surveys, the preexisting one and the one that was to replace it. Only after they had run both

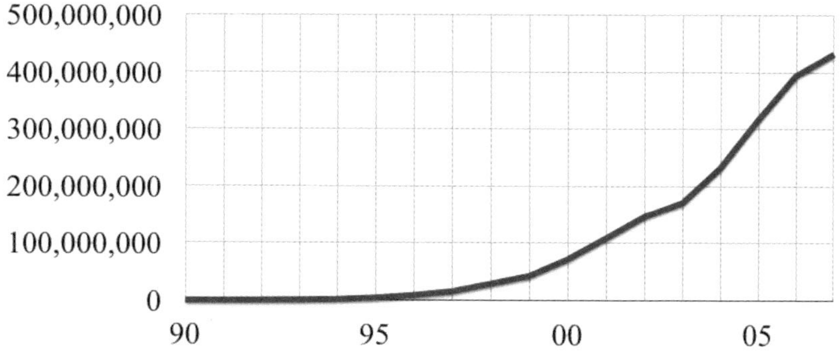

Figure 26: Estimated size of Internet, 1991-2007, by ISC

[31] ISC Domain Survey: Number of Internet Hosts, www.isc.org/index.pl?/ops/ds/host-count-history.php

alongside for thirty months (2.5 years) did they swap over and, in the process, change the numbers for the overlap interval so as to re-calibrate the old trend curve to the new regime. They did not simply drop the one and take up the other. To just jump abruptly is almost always malpractice as it both breaks the continuity of the trend line and loses any chance of calibration (error correction) in either the old or the new method. When you measure something as wiggly as "security," you will have to change measurement regimes from time to time but as with the ISC, it is good practice to maintain the trend curve by running both measures for a period of overlap.

There are many examples where this might come up with data security. For example, you might want to change your definition of what is forbidden in outbound e-mail as detected by one or another content filters. It would be wise to filter in two stages for a while to see what you had been missing, and to find an adjustment factor that allows you to re-scale the trendline leading up to the present time to what you will use going forward. Say your new filter knocks off another 5% of the outbound e-mail, and make the assumption that introducing the filter can only reduce that 5% figure; then your old curve of should-be-blocked can be scaled up by $1/.95 = +5.3\%$ and you can proceed forward with an unbroken record.

6.2. Measurement as score keeping

One of the big reasons to measure anything is to improve, and data security performance, like performance in any other game, is hard to improve without keeping score. Within our narrow focus of data security, there are many areas where keeping score makes sense.

Note that keeping score may well be an interval or even a ratio scale while it is being done, but it is inherently an ordinal scale by the time it enters into the record book. Using baseball as a model, a team does not have to have the highest aggregate run total to win its division, it just has to beat the other teams. It can win 50 games by one run each and lose one game by 100 runs and still come out on top. After winning the division, no one will much remember how they won, only that they were better than the others. Baseball counts runs to put the teams in order in a given game ($X > Y$), it then uses games to put the teams in order in the eligibility for the post season (best four records regardless of what those records were), and several layers later, it gets to a final ordering where position #1 is pretty much what matters. Horse racing is even more a matter of ordering where, oddly, the precision is in the payoff and that payoff has no relationship whatsoever to by how much horse #1 beat horse #2 beat horse #3...

Turning directly to data security, score keeping is probably best used in precisely the way it is used in baseball or horse racing, to put things in order. Suppose you have a monitoring tool that logs (some fraction of) all data events of an unhappy sort. You might have a policy against transferring whole folders to USB (removable) "disk drives" and so you may begin to get counts of such events. Now, suppose you have a security awareness program. As you have probably already guessed, one way to keep score is to pull from the log the records of when someone transfers a whole folder to a USB thumbdrive, but to express it as a rate at which such things happen, such as number of such transfers per day. Now you would look to see if that rate changes at or shortly after your awareness training happens and, if it does change, whether it reverts to pre-training levels and by when. By seeing if you get a change at all, you are looking at which is better, the company with or the company without training. This is a purely ordinal question, but it is data security decision support because by putting in order the company's performance with and without training, you know whether or not to bother. Note that this decision (so far) is whether things get better or do not get better, whether with training things are safer or are not more safe.

Now suppose that you keep that logging running. You might be able to say that whereas training does make the score better enough to prefer a trained company to untrained one, that the rate of whole folder transfer to USB microdrives falls back to the pre-training level after eighteen months. Again, and without knowing if you are catching all events, you can say now say that a company trained within the last eighteen months is better than one that has not been. Of course, this will lead you to re-train at least that often.

Of course, you can separate your logs into department by department rates and allow that to steer who gets training first. You can even do this at the individual level within or across departments. In all of this, the decisions of whether or not to do something do not depend on having a ratio scale (where you could say "Dept X is 3.7 times as good as Dept Y") or even an interval scale (where you could say that "Training made twice as much difference to Dept X as it did to Dept Y"), just an ordinal scale. The others are nice, but to begin at the beginning, your first attempts at measuring correlates of data security ought probably to aim at getting everything in order. That is the point, if you don't keep score, then your game cannot improve, and you can't keep score unless you have some sort of logging that is consistent enough that whatever errors logging itself makes are by and large the same errors day to day, event to event.

That condition of consistent error lets even your rudimentary first steps at measuring data security issues yield fruit because it allows comparisons, comparisons based on order ("Is $X > Y$?"). Those comparisons let you feed something into your decision making you will not have had before, the ability to know where to put your effort and to know if it had an effect when you did.

6.3. Measurement as predictive tool

When we measure data security over time, or anything else, and we at least have the condition where errors of measurement are not correlated with the outcome itself, the trendlines we get let us make decisions. They may also let us make modest prediction. As we discussed elsewhere, if your workfactor as a defender is rising very much faster than the workfactor of the attacker, either you have to have very deep pockets indeed or the attacker is going to win, and extending the shape of the existing curve makes that obvious. Forecasting in data security, or any digital security area, is nowhere near ready for prime time and may never be ready in the way that, say, life insurance underwriting is very ready to specify your odds of dying this month with five-digit accuracy.

One of the recent changes in the way in which data security is handled has been the so-called notification laws beginning with California's "SB1386."[32] The folks at Attrition have been tracking disclosed data losses for a while now.[33] After a bit of manipulation, we might be able to answer a question like "Are data loss events becoming more common?" As seen in Figure 27, the answer is clear that reports of data loss are becoming

---

[32] Assemblyman Joe Simitian introduced this as AB700, but a Senator took it over from him. It was Simitian's advisor, Deirdre Mulligan of Stanford, who modeled the bill on disclosure law around toxic waste spills.

[33] See `attrition.org/dataloss/` for more.

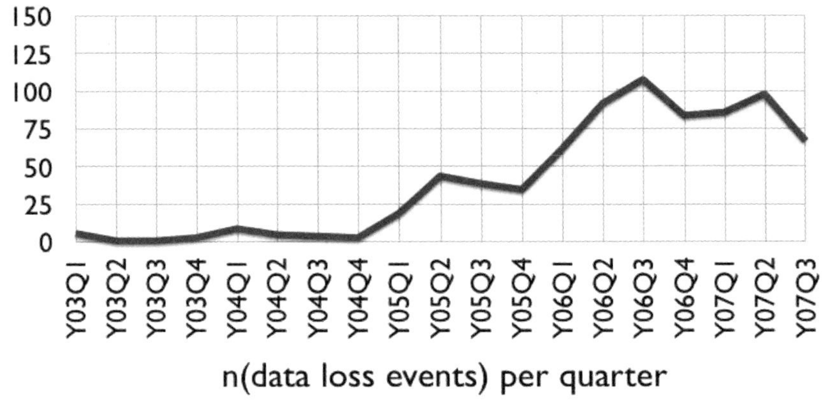

Figure 27: Number of data loss events reported per quarter, 2003-2007

more common but are still highly variable. Not shown is that the size of data loss events is even more highly variable — too much so to draw a meaningful graph, though "the number affected" is growing pretty steadily and may be accelerating. This is not good news, but as always when a reporting mandate enters the scene there is a period in which changes in the reporting fraction are part of what is going on and SB 1386 became effective in California (only) in July, 2003. And on that point, the 2005 CSI/FBI survey asked how many firms are willing to disclose absent a legal mandate, and came up with the figure 20%. Their 2007 survey confirmed this as the rate of non-response even to the CSI/FBI survey itself was falling so fast that parts of the survey were being dropped.[34] We therefore must look at Figure 27 with some scepticism. Nevertheless, the curve is striking and thus begs the question of "What next?" Here is where a little forecasting might help. First, we fit a line and see how good a fit we can get, then, second, we take the equation of the fitted line and we forecast a bit into the future. For the first part, get something like Figure 28, which fits well enough (correlation is .8892) that we can comfortably guess that for Y07Q4 we should expect 116 data loss events and, for Y08Q1, 127, as shown in Figure 29.

By the time this chapter is read, those dates will have come and gone and this gives us a second

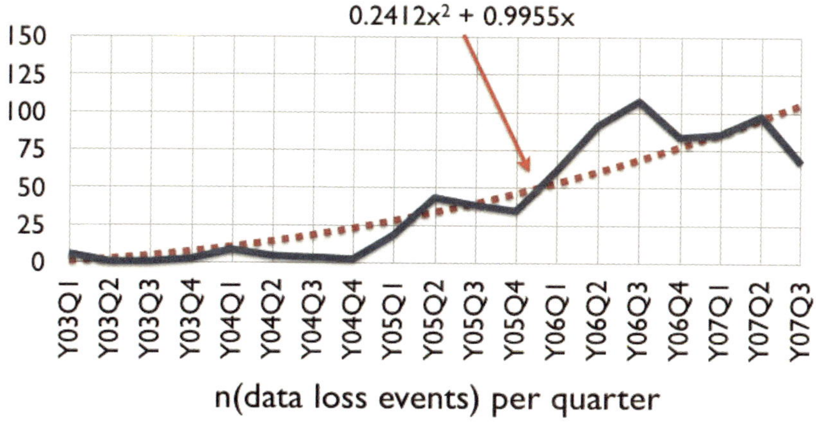

Figure 28: Simple model for data loss events per quarter

[34] Surveys available through `www.gocsi.com/forms/fbi/csi_fbi_survey.jhtm`

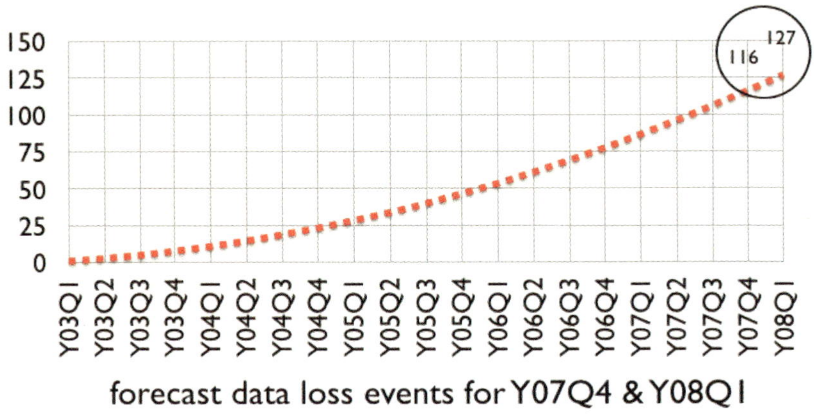

Figure 29: Forecast data loss events for two quarters out

advantage: we can tell if the forecasting is any good, or whether the rise in reported data loss incidents is just a reporting anomaly or something more important underlying that.

By no means is this enough, but perhaps you will agree that one of the values of measurement in and around data security is the ability to predict the future somewhat. That is why one of the definitions of "security" itself is "The absence of surprise." If we can predict, then we've no right to be surprised.

6.4. Measurement for decision support

Security metrics have no purpose if they do not support decision making for the purpose of managing risk. That is true for data security; we measure so that we can make decisions that manage the risks which threaten our data. This brings us to ask ourselves, "What risk management decisions would we make differently if we had some measurements to support our decision making?" That is why we are here.

So let's work another example. In this case, we'll look at the question of legal liability for data loss, disclaiming (of course) that the present author has any legal skill. The classic definition of liability comes from Judge Learned Hand who said, in paraphrase, that if it is more cost effective to anticipate and thus prevent a failure than it is to bear the risk, then there is liability for not having done so. This is a precedential case[35] for all of U.S. liability case law. He even spelled it out in arithmetic terms. Given

P	=	the probability of loss
L	=	the amount of said loss
B	=	the cost of adequate precautions

Then there is Liability whenever $B < PL$. That is simple enough, so let's apply it to a topic *du jour*: identity loss.

Applying Hand's calculus to 2003 data from the Federal Trade Commission[36] on identity theft, 4.6% of the population has suffered an identity fraud. In the process, they spent three hundred million hours

[35] UNITED STATES et al. v. CARROLL TOWING CO., Inc., et al.; Nos. 96, 97, Dockets 20371, 20372; SECOND CIRCUIT COURT OF APPEALS; 159 F.2d 169; January 9, 1947.

[36] Identity Theft Survey Report, Federal Trade Commission, September, 2003, as found at www.ftc.gov/os/2003/09/synovatereport.pdf

repairing the troubles caused (converted to dollars here at the 2003 Federal minimum wage) and they also spent five billion dollars out of pocket. The ten million people involved thus had a $655 loss per incident. Since the probability (P) of a loss, 4.6%, times the loss (L) of $655 imposes a burden (B) of $30.11, the question then is whether it is possible to protect an individual against identity fraud for $30.11 per annum. If it is, then liability is found. If not, not. In equation form, this is

$$P = 4.6\%$$

$$L = \frac{3 \times 10^8 hr \times \$5.15/hr + \$5x10^9}{10^7 victims} = \$655/victim$$

$$P \times L = \$30.11 = cutoff$$

We do not warrant this to be a true test of what is the liability risk, but this is what we mean by having security metrics as decision support. In this case, the metrics are the FTC numbers and the decision is whether you want to make a bet that this algebra will hold versus a bet that you can prevent identity fraud for $30.11 per potential victim. Not in any way to pick on them, but during January, 2007, TJX, Inc., announced the exposure of confidential information for 45,700,000 individuals. That is, at least in potential terms and using the FTC figures,

$$45{,}700{,}000\ persons * \$655/person = \$29{,}933{,}500{,}000$$

of exposure for the people involved, which we'll call $30B for convenience. If that is the loss potential, then even a 1-in-1000 chance of occurrence would imply that a $30M security program ought to have been in place.

For an entirely different example of decision support, let's borrow the ideas behind public health vaccination campaigns and apply them to emergency security patching procedures. In the public health arena, vaccination (patching) is never fully effective, either because of not getting 100% coverage or because the vaccine is not 100% effective. And, of course, there is often not enough vaccine to go around. In that public health situation, one is left with a choice of whether to steer the vaccination program by impact reduction or by transmission suppression.

- If vaccinating against harm, then you supply the vaccine to those who would suffer most. In health, the sick and the weak get first intervention. In security, the juiciest targets (data or control) get first intervention. Scoring this is by relative risk of harm measured before and after, or at milestone intervals.
- If vaccinating against transmission, the term of art is "herd immunity" which means what it sounds like — making the herd immune rather than the individual. In the real world, you vaccinate those most likely to transmit such as care givers themselves. In security, machines with the greatest number of connectable counterparties (perhaps instant messaging servers, say), might get the vaccine (patch) first.

In either case, you are managing risk. To do that you have to have some sense of what you are willing to lose. In the public health arena, it is the tradeoff between mortality of the weak and morbidity of the many. In the security arena, it will come down to what your ends really are — and security is not your end.

Say, for example, that while security is not an end that data integrity is (an end). If the nature of the threat is poisoning your data, and if you are lucky enough to know approximately where in the data stream the poisoning occurs if it can occur at all, then obviously you marshall your resources to not put any more bad data into the stream and you do this before you try to clean up whatever bad data is already in the stream.

As a different example, suppose the threat is exfiltration of data that you know lives in a fixed number of locations. You might first close the border the way the police might cordon off a city block, and then you might visit every place that data lives to do some additional lockdown.

Suppose that availability of your data is paramount. It may be of very short lived utility, like a stock ticker near the close of the trading day, so loss of confidentiality, while important, has *de minimus* lasting impact whereas loss of data availability is a firing offense for whole teams. For this, there is an equation:

$$Availability = \frac{MTBF}{MTBF + MTTR}$$

where

$$MTBF = MeanTimeBetweenFailure$$

and

$$MTTR = MeanTimeToRepair$$

In words, you get 100% Availability if either the MTBF is infinite (nothing ever breaks) or the MTTR is zero (recovery is instant).

$$A = 1 = \begin{cases} \dfrac{\infty}{\infty + MTTR} \\ \dfrac{MTBF}{MTBF + 0} \end{cases}$$

So, if you are the data security planner, then you have some tradeoffs between investing heavily in MTBF increase or in MTTR reduction. Most likely, whatever investments you can make will have diminishing returns at some level of expenditure and so you come to a tradeoff. Unless you are doing some measurement of money in and failure rates out, you are likely to either over-spend or under-protect.

Adi Shamir, the "S" of "RSA," received the Turing Award in 2004. His acceptance lecture[37] included three points that are directly relevant to data security:

---

[37] www.acm.org/awards/turing_lectures_project/turing/S/s-pp/shamir_1files_files/TextOnly/index.html

- Absolutely secure systems do not exist
- To halve your vulnerability, you have to double your expenditure
- Cryptography is typically bypassed, not penetrated

and that, too, reminds us of the data security problem. In particular, the second of the three bullets is why tradeoffs such as between herd immunity and harm reduction, between failure prevention and fast recovery, and, more simply, between bearing a risk versus diminishing that risk require measurement. You have to know your risks or you will find yourself walking down the garden path, such as rediscovering that if your risks are uncorrelated, then redundancy raises Availability but if your risks are correlated, then redundancy lowers Availability. (Planting yet more acreage in susceptible corn does not lower disease risk, it raises it.)

6.5. Specifics unique to data and its measurement

So what, in particular, do we need to do when we are looking at data security. What might we measure and where might we stand to take those measurements? A balanced scorecard is a now-standard part of business planning, albeit not for security, so let's start by picking a high goal: *viz.*, a "balanced scorecard" for data secu-

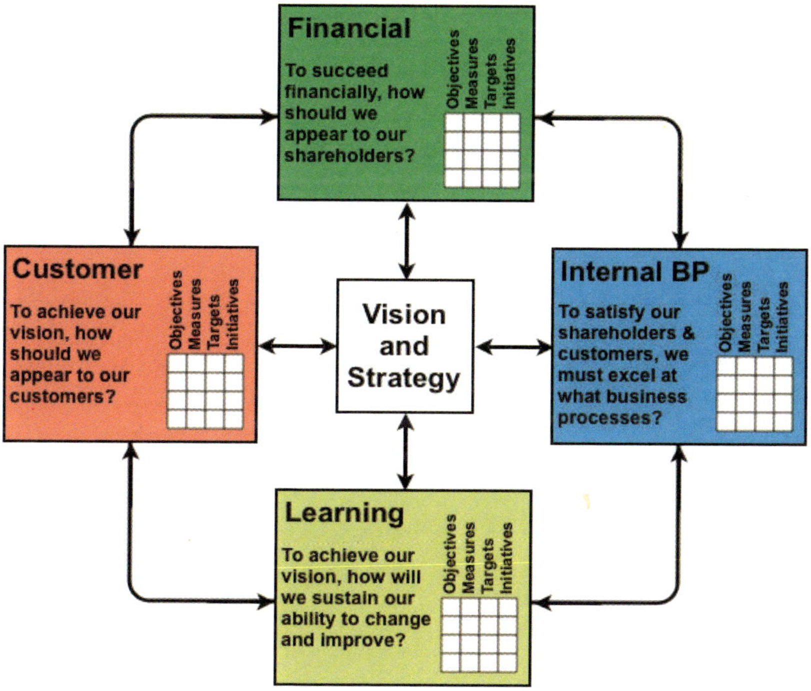

Figure 30: The Balanced Scorecard

rity. The balanced scorecard[38] looks like Figure 30. and while there is definitely insufficient space in this book to detail the entire balanced scorecard strategy and system of metrics, we can say what sort of things would appear in a balanced data security scorecard. In other settings, balanced scorecards can and often are combined

[38] Kaplan RS & Norton DP : "The Balanced Scorecard: Measures That Drive Performance," Harvard Business Review, January-February 1992; see www.balancedscorecard.org/

("rolled up") and one would hope that a balanced data security scorecard would roll its way to the top of the corporation.

So how do we do this? How do we construct a balanced scorecard with security in mind? There seems to be little to no prior art here though, as always, some company somewhere is probably already doing this. But our question, knowing what we know, is how does the financial view interact with security? How does the business process view interact with security? How does the learning and growth view interact with security? How does the customer view interact with security?

Besides the somewhat silly answer of "However you want it to interact with security," it is not clear where this ends up, but it is becoming clear where to start. A 2006 book by Andrew Jaquith,[39] has a good starting point, which, with modifications, would be as follows:

6.5.1. Financial view

The financial view answers the question "To succeed financially, how should we appear to our shareholders?" The kinds of goals that contribute to being viewed favorably along the financial axis have significant interplay with data security. Priority one is to ensure that revenue-generation does, in fact, proceed

[39] Jaquith AR, Security Metrics, Addison-Wesley, 2006.

unimpeded by data security lapses, one would probably very much be interested in preserving the integrity of needed records as well, mechanisms to generally achieve lower risk for the revenue generators would seem attractive at all times, and if, as with most mature industries, reliability is *the* high goal, then measuring data security's contributions to reliability seems desirable. The kinds of data security metrics that would be germane to goals like these might include:

Cost of data security per transaction
Downtimes lost to attack by attack classes
Data flow per transaction & per source
Budget correlation with risk measures

The reasons for choosing these are two-fold; first, they can be gotten and, second, they have some leverage, which is to say they can heighten the contrasts of what they measure, thus helping decision making to proceed.

Data security can be priced as a cost and that cost allocated over all transactions to which it applies thus deriving a cost of data security per transaction. Such a figure is inherently normalized to something that is well understood, *viz.*, the unit of one transaction, and other statistics related to core transaction can be brought into play. In a similar way, data flows per source per transaction can be derived and, combined with the data security cost per transaction, can achieve further leverage by sorting transaction types both by the volume of data they involve and the costs of protection per unit of protection, per unit of production, or other financial calibration. If data loss is ongoing, then classifying it along as many dimensions as it is practical to do will lead to improved understanding of the differences between transactions that justify a high level of data security cost per unit of transaction-relevant data and those which require less. If risk measures are available, and over time they must be made to be available, then the correlation (or lack thereof) between risk measures and mitigating countermeasures will certainly need calibration.

The usual difficulty for any (budgetary) security allocation is how to price protection. Therefore, a scorecard that shows how protection is being applied, calibrated by both risk and per-transaction measures, will certainly be the kind of roll-up information of interest to the C-level executive.

6.5.2. Business process view

Here we ask what business processes are needed to satisfy both the shareholders and the customers. While "satisfy" is certainly context specific, data security figures into the processes involved and throughout. First, it is important to minimize those unknown unknowns. With data, this is perhaps the paramount concern as data, stored as bits, does not have an exclusion principle the way a physical object does. While you would likely notice the theft of your car or your pants, the theft of your data leaves no vacuum and so the unknown unknown, *viz.*, that you have lost data, does not ever present itself until such time as you may chance to stumble over the misuse of the data that you did not, until that moment, realize had gone missing. Any process that helps to minimize the number and scope of unknown unknowns is therefore valuable for the business process view and should factor into the scorecard for it. Concurrently, the protection of information assets against known threats is essential; customers and shareholders are likely to be especially miffed if you get knocked over by some commonplace attack. The principles of Least-Privilege and Need-to-Know are likely to be appropriate throughout your business processes if you want to limit exposure to insider problems. Finally, some forms of verification & accreditation of your business processes will work to satisfy your shareholders and customers. The kinds of data security metrics that would be germane to this second set of goals might include:

Percentage of critical systems under a DR plan
Percentage of systems obeying ______ policy
MTBF & MTTR for security incidents
Frequency of security team internal consultations
Latency to obey ______ change orders, by dept.

As before, these suggestions will increase the leverage your metrics have on decision makers within the business.

Assuming for the moment that you know which systems are critical, it is an obvious jump to look at the percentage of those critical systems which have a workable disaster recovery (DR) plan. Similarly, the number of systems that do obey a given security policy divided by the number that should will yield a useful metric. Put differently, while it is both trendy and accurate to say that the enterprise has no real perimeter, for the purpose of this discussion it might be better to say that the enterprise's perimeter is operationally defined by the reach of its policies (thus making the percentage of systems that obey policy a measure of the enterprise itself). For security incidents, the availability calculus mentioned earlier applies and the time between incidents and the time to recover from them are both useful metrics and more useful still in combination. Because it has long been shown that a central security team cannot do the job of enterprise protection without the assistance of security teams throughout the organization, a metric on the business process that measures that assistance, *viz.*, the rate and number of times the central team is brought in by business unit teams is worth measuring. Finally, recognizing that in the matters of data security time is often of the essence as threats change daily, the latency of mitigations is an important metric. (Latency may be the most important of all, in fact, and because of this may well drive solution choice when it comes time to buy product.)

6.5.3. Learning & growth view

The idea of a learning and growth view is that the enterprise can be greater than the sum of its parts, but not by accident. Harder to measure than some other aspects, but security awareness and security culture generally need attention and transparency if the enterprise is to have the security assistance of more than just a few job descriptions. This may include some degree of certification, although certification programs are generally a lowest common denominator screening exercise. Training is more the key, but training can be tied to the rigor of certification such as may be available. Levels of collaboration, especially early engagement with outside peers and groups, is a sign of the kind of awareness that has to be in place later if not sooner.

Example data security related metrics to get at the elusive matters of learning and growth might include:

Percentage of job reviews involving security
Percentage of security workers with training
Ratio of b.u. security staff to central staff
Timely new system security consultations
Percentage of programs with budgeted security

A simple calculation of the percentage of job reviews involving security is actually quite meaningful as a job review is both the time and place to do recalibration of the expectations of the enterprise and the employee both to each other. The percentage of security workers with training (and current skill) is another scoring metric. Looking at metrics with more leverage, rather than the simple counts of the number of security staff in the core of the enterprise and in the peripheral business units, the ratio of business unit security staff to central staff will tend to mirror the degree to which data security is taken seriously in those business units. The rate (number per unit time interval) of timely security consultations between central staff and the peripheral business units, broken out by which side initiated the discussion, will also get the measurer closer to knowing if the data security message is getting through. If the enterprise is the sort where every attempt to measure the importance of an issue comes back to budget numbers, then, of course, the percentage of programs with budgeted security interventions is the obvious answer, again broken out in every way that makes sense organizationally and risk-wise.

6.5.4. Customer view

Customers, quite naturally, do not want to think about security so when they do it is likely that it comes with demands on you that are unfriendly and very much in the present. To help with the customer view of data security, it is important to decrease security backscatter (or perhaps we should say "insecurity backscatter") in the sense that having customers contact you because of reported insecurity problems, whether those contacts are well founded or not, is something to be avoided. You need to find a way to increase the options for business with you that the customer has but without increasing risk, real or imagined, for that customer. The world being as it is, customer-visible regulatory compliance and the proof thereof is not a question of whether but a question of how, and of cost effectiveness. As always, for a mature industry reliability is an implicit measure by which your customers will judge you. Security is, or can be, a contributor to reliability (just as insecurity can be a contributor to unreliability), and therefore this falls under the "customer view" part of the balanced scorecard.

Example metrics to get at the customer view would likely include, at least,

Percentage of SLAs with security standards
Percentage of tested external-facing apps
Number of non-employees with access
Percentage of data secure-by-default
Percentage of customer data outside data center

The idea of continuous improvement will have to include a simple count of the percentage of service level agreements (SLAs) that include data security standards, as that both signals to the customer that your firm takes it seriously as well as taking unpredictability out of the system. This is so important that we'll pause for couple of paragraphs on that alone.

Attorney Jeffrey Ritter,[40] is a persuasive spokesman for the proposition that data security is a fundamental differentiator amongst firms. When he characterizes the (legal) risk to firms today, he does so quite succinctly:

---

[40] His firm is Waters Edge Consulting, at `wec-llc.com/`

> That which was not recorded did not happen.
> That which is not documented does not exist.
> That which has not been tested is insecure.

which he does not mean as "Here is how to be invisible" but rather what believable evidence has to mean by the time someone gets to the witness stand. To be believable, proto-evidence has to be a direct record about something that is itself documented, and the process by which the digital records came to be presented in court has to be able to withstand a challenge that its veracity is suspect and especially so unless attempts to defeat its integrity protection have been already and duly made (and themselves recorded and documented). Yes, nearly all the data we handle will never by called into a question in a courtroom, but it is good to know the evolving issues as exactly which data might be subject to discovery changes without notice. In the U.S., the so-called E-Discovery rules[41] that went into effect in December, 2006, are the case in point (as lightly discussed elsewhere).

Along Ritter's lines, the purposes of the customer view will be much advanced by any increase in the percentage of external-facing applications that have been tested by competent third parties. Just knowing the number of non-employees with privileged access, whether they are consultants or outsourcers, is an

---

[41] Many sources of further information, of which this is an example: www.uscourts.gov/rules/Reports/ST09-2006.pdf

essential metric for, if nothing else, what the limit of your expectations should be for making all your direct employees into perfect angels. The percentage of data that is secure-by-default, and this includes data within software products that you purchase from others, is, like the number of non-employees with privileged access, a bounding box for how good things can be if all you do is run things as they come from the manufacturer using employees who never do anything wrong. Finally, if you do not know the percentage of customer data that is outside the data center, then you will never be able to say what the protection status of that customer data is, and the customer will not be amused.

6.5.5. How to get this to fly

This is a book about data security, but data security, if it is to be real, has to be a pervasive concern and practice. Scorecards such as the one described earlier are necessary, but they are not sufficient just because they were made or just because some part of central security staff is aware of their content and meaning. No, and as said at the outset, the scorecards have to eventually roll up to the highest levels of management. There is no formula the present author can give that is a one size for all, but what can be said is that the rolling up (or cascading down, if you prefer) of the scorecards has a very important side effect, one almost valuable enough to justify the work of the scorecards themselves: Cascading scorecards build bridges. Those bridges between entities of the organization that are tied together by data security — tied because they share the responsibility or because they share the downside risk — those bridges must be built. The use of a scorecard mechanism, where the the results in one department and the results in another are combined in a visible way, is extremely valuable specifically because it makes the theoretic real and it is essentially transparent.

Of course, when you measure something with management implications there is eventually going to be some accountability for what was measured. Frankly, it is high time that data security had some accountability wrapped around it; to move forward we need the accountability and to get the accountability we need numbers. That doesn't mean that we don't accept some risks, but the numbers can and must become a sorting mechanism between risks we bear and risks we mitigate, with the data security metrics a kind of arbiter between accountability and bad luck. That we are even having this conversation says that accountability, and the numbers that backstop it, is an idea whose time has come.

When a scorecard of any sort is introduced, it (like software) needs a field (β) test to see if it works as expected. This is really pretty important as measurements, whether we like it or not, take on a life of their own so it would be wise to get them right enough at the outset to live with them afterwards. Again, this is not the book to read for how to introduce a data security scorecard, but in any case the scorecard you want is one where a cause and an effect can be linked to the working satisfaction of all concerned. The reason we are doing a scorecard, if indeed you do, is to connect cause and effect and then, just as Borge's canon of risk management says, to change the future, not to explain the past. If we do that — if we are able to show a cause producing a future changing effect — then we can counter the idea that security is reactive and only reactive. In data security more than anywhere else, a purely reactive model is a guarantee of failure; data lost is never data found, data exposed is never data unrevealed, data poisoned is never data trusted, and so forth.

Though it is unlikely to be possible today, we are soon coming to a world where a firm's data security is rated. In the financial world, entities such as Standard & Poors and Moody's Investor Services rate the risk, reward, and predictability of financial instruments. Financial instruments without such ratings are thus suspect, and the rating mechanism is transparent, funded by the ratee, and oft-revised. If one believes that data is very nearly the coin of the digital world, and that what happens in finance will continue to presage what happens in other fields, it only stands to reason that software will get safety ratings just like bonds (or toaster ovens) and that data handling will subsequently follow. This will not happen overnight nor should you wait for it to do so, but as a bit of crystal ball fortune telling, data that is valuable is data for which its containment must eventually be rated. As 2007 draws to a close, security ratings have come to application software; can data be far behind?

In the meantime, every person worried with data security wants to know the answers to these questions

How secure am I?
Am I better off than last year?
Am I spending just enough?
How do I compare to my peers?
Is risk transfer preferable?

Every one of those requires numbers, numbers that either come from homegrown measurements valuable to a scorecard approach or which come from benchmarks set by others. Comparing yourself to others will be done, so you may want to do it first and see if your efforts are over-spending or under-protecting.

In sum, data security is no longer a-nice-to-have, it is a die-without, and unless and until you have data security embedded in all of the management chain you are subject to surprise. Put differently,

The operational definition of
security is
"No Surprises."

7. The nature of the market

The market for data security is no more static than the threat, though one must understand that the opponents can devise mechanisms for data theft faster than defenders can do a good job of building and deploying protective mechanisms. It is almost impossible for investors in digital security companies to understand what those companies do. Few, if any, information security officers actually command their companies in the way a quality control officer can shut down a production line. No General Counsel really wants to know about all the potential data security problems the firm might have as, on the one hand, there are too many to solve while, on the other hand, knowing there was a problem before bad things happened is the recipe for liability judgments. Government cannot lead; in fact, it can barely follow as procurement inertia in the face of fast mutating threat yields the only fruit it can, reactive, not proactive, investment. The public is frightened but inured, worried but addicted to the electronic conveniences though those of significant wealth want protection from the 'net as much as they want protection from panhandlers and papparazi. Nearly everyone believes in miracles, and few there are who both understand what they manage and manage what they understand. If that sounds like Hunter Thompson, so be it, but let's try to get some value down on paper.

7.1. Technical and business justifications never match

When looking at why enterprises buy security products, it is very much the last plaint above that drives: Technology is dominated by those who manage what they do not understand and who understand what they do not manage. You can see this, transparently actually, in the plethora of point products, each of which cures this or that problem but none of which get ahead of the curve. The reason is that the business justifications for purchase and installation rarely match the technical justifications. This is not an indictment of anyone; it is, rather, a fact of nature.

Take an historical example, the installation of firewalls. The technical reason for putting them in probably could be summed up with something that security people, *per se*, would be comfortable with — the preservation of network and service integrity in the face of burgeoning vandalism. The business reason had nothing to do with details like "network integrity" but rather with something like making clear where inside and outside was so that inside the command structure's directives could be made to hold. Sure, that description can be argued with, but "What do I get for this?" has different answers if your view is framed by the financial and market position of the firm versus a view framed by trading off installation difficulty to firefighting difficulty. In other words, digital security is like so many other human endeavors, where you stand depends on where you sit.

We should all hope for better, however, and it appears that the key to "better" is for each side, the technical and the business, to come closer to speaking each other's language. This book is not a paean to corporate change agents or anything of that sort, but we'll all be better off if the business side sees that technical risk management is a real issue just as if the technical side sees that business risk management is likewise a real issue.

For the business side, the most important realization is that data is a rising fraction of total corporate wealth. We've had three decades of rising investment in information technology while the value per dollar has doubled over and over again,[42] like clockwork, at a rate that approximates one percent per week (.89%/wk, see Figure 31)

---

[42] Graph from `www.intel.com/technology/mooreslaw/pix/mooreslaw_graph2.gif`

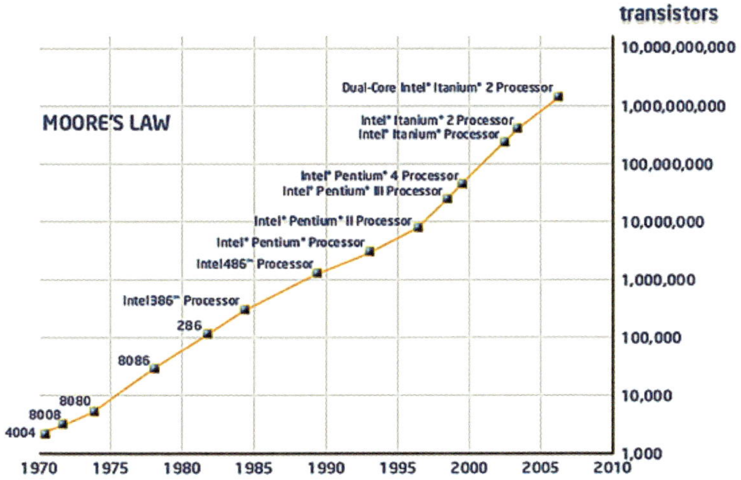

Figure 31: Moore's Law, +1%/wk

while over those same three decades, the broad measure of total corporate wealth embodied in the Dow Jones Industrial Average (DJIA) has likewise risen,[43] but at a rate that approximates one seventh of one percent per week (0.14%/wk, see Figure 32). From that, the business side of the house has to admit that either all that investment in data storage, data processing, and data transmission equipment has been wasted, that the unit value of data is falling seven-fold per week, or that data is a growing fraction of total corporate assets. If the business side is not only aware but also looking ahead, they should imagine a day when intangible property

[43] Graph from `www.analyzeindices.com/dow-jones-history.shtml`

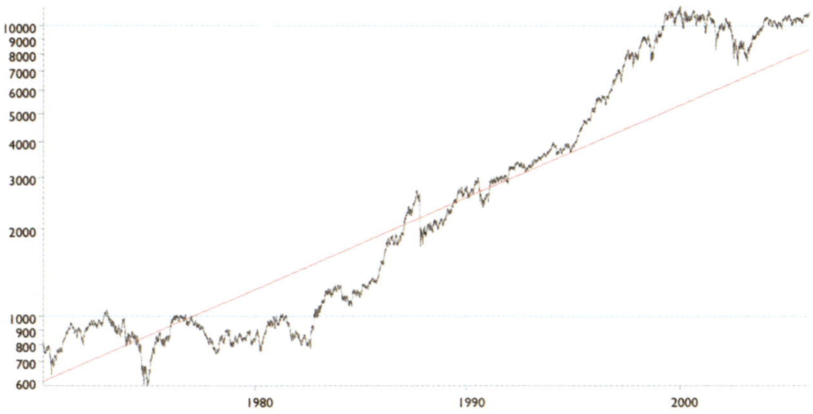

Figure 32: DJIA, +0.14%/wk

dominates the corporate balance sheet and is required by law to be valued there. When that happens, *viz.*, when intangible property must appear on the balance sheet, then two things will happen. First, CFOs will have to price the corporate data assets in some way that will survive audit. Second, Boards will have to include data protection policy and performance within their purview as the ultimate overseers of the stockholders' assets.

For the technical side, it has to learn, and learn well, the four verities of governance:

> Most important ideas are not interesting,
> Most interesting ideas are not important,
> Not every problem has a good solution, &
> Every solution has side effects.

Most will say that they already know this, but they don't insofar as expressing what is technically interesting is almost always of no value to driving a business while that which makes a business hum, reliability for example, is almost by definition going to be boring. For reliability, Boring is Good. What is perhaps hardest is how every solution has side effects insofar as side effects due to the technical sphere may be felt in the business sphere, and vice versa. No digital security product, for example, is even conceivable if it requires the enterprise be upgraded en massé. From a technical point of view, lock-step upgrades are much preferred but from a business point of view the cost of having even a moment of lock-step is absurdly high.

- Technical folks and business folks will probably find it easiest to cooperate when it comes to disaster recovery as in those circumstances the technical folks will be able to get across how the recovery will not be all or nothing but incremental while the business folks will be able to get across what functions are more important than others.
- Where the two sides are clearly talking different languages might be in the area of encryption; the business folks see it as a risk management exercise

aimed at avoiding legal and market risk. The Technical folks see it differently, and they understand that encrypting everything moves the risk of loss from stolen laptops to the difficulty of crafting key management regimes that scale but don't get in the way.

Note that where regulation is pervasive, the business idea of spending only as much as would be needed (to later be seen to have been prudent) meets the technical idea that instrumentation makes technical management possible. To show that your firm is, generally speaking, doing the "best practices" thing, you need some record keeping and some automatic alarms and alerts. These are nearly always valuable just for technical management reasons alone, so this is another area where the business and technical folks can find common ground.

Other than this sort of "start with where you are, not with where you want to be," there is not a lot more to say since if there is nothing in common there is nothing to say. The bottom line, though, for both the technical person wanting to justify a technical innovation and the business person wanting to justify a business innovation is that data and the protection of it is where they will find common ground. Data is where the value is and data is where the risk is. Risk to that value motivates business decisions. Value from addressing risks motivates technical decisions. For once, we all have something to talk about.

7.2. Market analysts cannot afford to pick winners on rational grounds

Like it says, market analysts cannot afford to pick winners on rational grounds. Why? The economics of analyst firms precludes it. Although the top analyst firms recognize that the integrity of their work is essential to their continued success, they face conflicts of interest that are comparable, and perhaps even a little more direct, to those faced by investment banks. Analyst firms have three primary sources of revenue — subscriptions from user companies, subscriptions from software vendors, and consulting (including speaking engagements), with the software vendors' share of revenue coming in circa 80%. Although consulting can be lucrative, it does not scale in the way that the subscription-based publishing business does, thus subscriptions tend to be the higher margin business and to drive the company's overall valuation.

As a result, the management team typically devises mechanisms internally to make individual analysts as responsible as possible for specific segments of subscription revenue. From a business perspective, this is completely as it should be. Individual analysts are goaled and often paid according to subscription revenue associated with their particular software or service segment.

An added complication stems from the way user companies purchase access to the firm's information.

Generally, these user subscriptions provide access to most of the firm's publications. Thus, the revenue associated with these subscriptions is spread across a wide range of software categories. Although the firm may apportion the revenue according to readership or inquiry rates of each software category, the reality is that this revenue is spread more or less evenly across all the analysts and individual analysts can do very little to impact user company subscription revenue.

Of course, the opposite is true of software vendor subscription revenue. Virtually all of it can be defined by software segment and attributed to individual analysts. As a result, total vendor subscription revenue in their particular software category often plays a significant role in both the performance evaluations and the compensation packages of individual analysts. This situation has similar moral hazards to financial research analysts charged with conducting disinterested evaluations of firms that may be doing large volumes of investment banking business.

In the analyst firms, despite the best intentions of both management and analysts to maintain a Chinese wall between the revenue and the firm's opinion — in spite of all the "nothing but the truth policies" — it is extraordinarily rare for an analyst to adopt a minority opinion in a particular software segment. To put it another way, if ten (10) firms are pursuing one technical approach and two (2) are pursuing another, the individual analysts will, perhaps understandably, rarely criticize the approach of the majority.

And lest it be thought that this is irrelevant harping about the analyst community, theirs is an impossible job but, given that many buyers of security technology and security buy based on what the analysts say to buy, it is only fair to ask what motivates the analysts. This is little different than the brilliant passage in the brilliant book, Freakonomics, where Levitt & Dubner show that real estate agents get better deals when they are selling their own properties than they get for you when you are selling yours. Why? Because they know things you don't, and because their reward structure matters where the advice they give you is concerned. Since data security is a whole more more important than the marginal profit of a home sale, it pays to understand the reward structure of those who tell you when and what to buy.

7.3. Complexity is the enemy vs. the added complexity in solutions

Many, including the present author, have said that "Complexity is the enemy of security" but none so much as Bruce Schneier, who begins his famous essay,[44] "Software Complexity and Security," with one line, "The future of digital systems is complexity, and complexity is the worst enemy of security," and ends it with another, "Unfortunately, simplicity goes against everything our digital future stands for." Between those two, he has a lot to say and, with permission, it seems best to

[44] Quoted by permission; original at `www.schneier.com/crypto-gram-0003.html`

let him speak for himself and in full. The quotation is long but relevant.

Software Complexity and Security

The future of digital systems is complexity, and complexity is the worst enemy of security.

Digital technology has been an unending series of innovations, unintended consequences, and surprises, and there's no reason to believe that will stop anytime soon. But there is one thing that has held constant through it all, and it's that digital systems have gotten more complicated.

We've seen it over the past several years. Microprocessors have gotten more complex. Operating systems have gotten more complex. Computers have gotten more complex. Networks have gotten more complex. Individual networks have combined, further increasing the complexity. I've said it before, but it's worth repeating: The Internet is probably the most complex machine mankind has ever built. And it's not getting any simpler anytime soon.

As a consumer, I think this complexity is great. There are more choices, more options, more things I can do. As a security professional, I think it's terrifying. Complexity is the worst enemy of security. This has been true since the beginning of computers, and is likely to be true for the foreseeable future. And as cyberspace continues to get more complex, it will continue to get less secure. There are several reasons why this is true.

The first reason is the number of security bugs. All software contains bugs. And as the complexity of the software goes up, the number of bugs goes up. And a percentage of these bugs will affect security. The second reason is the modularity of complex systems. Complex systems are necessarily modular; there's no other way to handle the complexity than by breaking it up into manageable pieces. We could never have made the Internet as complex and interesting as it is today without modularity. But increased modularity means increased security flaws, because security often fails where two modules interact.

We've already seen examples of this as everything becomes Internet-aware. For years we knew that Internet applications like sendmail and rlogin had to be secure, but the recent epidemic of macro viruses shows that Microsoft Word and Excel need to be secure. Java applets not only need to be secure for the uses they are intended, they also need to be secure for any other use an attacker might think of. Photocopiers, maintenance ports on routers, mass storage units: these can all be made Internet-aware, with the associated security risks. Rogue printer drivers can compromise Windows NT. Malicious e-mail attachments can tunnel through firewalls. Convenience features in Microsoft Outlook can compromise security.

The third reason is the increased testing requirements for complex systems. I've talked elsewhere about security and failure testing. The only reasonable way to test the security of a system is to perform security evaluations on it. However, the more complex the system is, the harder a security evaluation becomes. A more complex system will have more security-related errors in the specification, design, and implementation. And unfortunately, the number of errors and the difficulty of evaluation does not grow in step with the complexity, but in fact grows much faster.

For the sake of simplicity, let's assume the system has ten different settings, each with two possible choices. Then there are 45 different pairs of choices that could interact in unexpected ways, and 1024 different configurations altogether. Each possible interaction can lead to a security weakness, and must be explicitly tested. Now, assume that the system has twenty different settings. This means 190 different pairs of choices, and about a million different configurations. Thirty different settings means 435 different pairs and a billion different configurations. Even slight increases in the complexity of systems mean an explosion in the number of different configurations ... any one of which could hide a security weakness.

The increased number of possible interactions creates more work during the security evaluation. For a system with a moderate number of options, checking all the two-option interactions becomes a huge amount of work. Checking every possible configuration is effectively impossible. Thus the difficulty of performing security evaluations also grows very rapidly with increasing complexity. The combination of additional (potential) weaknesses and a more difficult security analysis unavoidably results in insecure systems.

The fourth reason is that the more complex a system is, the harder it is to understand. There are all sorts of vulnerability points — human-computer interface, system interactions — that become much larger when you can't keep the entire system in your head.

The fifth (and final) reason is the difficulty of analysis. The more complex a system is, the harder it is to do this kind of analysis. Everything is more complicated: the specification, the design, the implementation, the use. And as we've seen again and again, everything is relevant to security analysis.

A more complex system loses on all fronts. It contains more weaknesses to start with, its modularity exacerbates those weaknesses, it's harder to test, it's harder to understand, and it's harder to analyze.

It gets worse: This increase in the number of security weaknesses interacts destructively with the weakest-link property of security: the security of the overall system is limited by the security of its weakest link. Any single weakness can destroy the security of the entire system. Real systems show no signs of becoming less complex. In fact, they are becoming more complex faster and faster. Microsoft Windows is a poster child for this trend to complexity. Windows 3.1, released in 1992, had 3 million lines of code; Windows 95 has 15 million and Windows 98 has 18 million. The original Windows NT (also 1992) had 4 million lines of code; NT 4.0 (1996) has 16.5 million. In 1998, Windows NT 5.0 was estimated to have 20 million lines of code; by the time it was renamed Windows 2000 (in 1999) it had between 35 million and 60 million lines of code, depending on who you believe.[45] *(As points of comparison, Solaris has held pretty stable at about 7 to 8 million lines of code for the last few releases, and*

[45] Vista has since ballooned to over 100 million.

Linux, even with the addition of X Windows and Apache, is still under 5 million lines of code.)

The size of Windows 2000 is absolutely amazing, and it will have more security bugs than Windows NT 4.0 and Windows 98 combined. In its defense, Microsoft has claimed that it spent 500 people-years to make Windows 2000 reliable. I only reprint this number because it will serve to illustrate how inadequate 500 people-years is.

The networks of the future, necessarily more complex, will be less secure. The technology industry is driven by demand for features, for options, for speed. There are no standards for quality or security, and there is no liability for insecure software. Hence, there is no economic incentive to create high quality. Instead, there is an economic incentive to create the lowest quality the market will bear. And unless customers demand higher quality and better security, this will never change.

I see two alternatives. The first is to recognize that the digital world will be one of ever-expanding features and options, of ever-faster product releases, of ever-increasing complexity, and of ever-decreasing security. This is the world we have today, and we can decide to embrace it knowingly.

The other choice is to slow down, to simplify, and to try to add security. Customers won't demand this — the issues are too complex for them to understand — so a consumer advocacy group is required. I can easily imagine an FDA-like organization for the Internet, but it can take a decade to approve a new prescription drug for sale, so this solution might not be economically viable.

I repeat: complexity is the worst enemy of security. Secure systems should be cut to the bone and made as simple as possible. There is no substitute for simplicity.

Unfortunately, simplicity goes against everything our digital future stands for.

Schneier's essay may seem like either old news, a lot to quote, or both, but while it was written in the year 2000, everything it said is still true and everything it predicted is now true, though even Schneier left out one thing worth remembering — every single security product increases the complexity of the system into which it is installed. And even if the core of the security product arrives in a simple (non-complex) form, it is often possible to configure it into a complex state.[46] So what are we to do?

One thing we have to do is to ensure that if such and such a function is not needed that it is turned off. Another is that complexity measures have a place in any security metrics program as, at least, a way to rank alternatives. Another is to operationally recognize that a software upgrade that is automatic and which adds features is going to add risk at least in proportion to the number of unwanted features. Perhaps most germane here is to stop installing one new security product for every new threat; that way lies madness.

---

[46] See, for example, Wool A, "A Quantitative Study of Firewall Configuration Errors," IEEE Computer, v37 n6 pp6-67, June, 2004, which discusses this very point in detail.

But let's be clear — there is a difficult tradeoff lurking here. Yes, security products add complexity, but as we discuss later on, this is not the entire story. The counter-pressure is that of the cost of integration. For applications, there is genuine economic value in having this application play nicely with that application as, for example, office productivity suites can and must do. This mutual or joint integration very much diminishes the cost of operations, and it is thus no wonder that suites long ago beat out best-of-breed for the commodity side of modern IT-centric business. But that integration comes at a complexity cost that is precisely where the security risk also comes from. How to balance the risk of a suite of applications all working well together but thereby sharing common-mode failure mechanisms with the risk of disparate applications that, by being different, do not have common-mode failure but, instead, have unique failure modes?

The trendy word is to "harden" applications, so using the language of material science, the question is thus whether the hardening one does within a suite is more like toughening or more like embrittlement? A hardened-in-the-sense-of-tough glass plate will accumulate (and show) all the scratches it's ever received, but it won't shatter. A hardened-in-the-sense-of-brittle glass plate won't accumulate (or show) any damage unless and until it is hit hard enough in which case it no longer is one piece of glass but several. Where is the greater risk? Is it John Wayne — scarred but still standing — or is it Superman — repulsing all until the

Kryptonite shows up. Perhaps the answer depends on how you read the next section.

7.4. Being future-proof

Everyone knows the threat evolves quickly and I've shown it often enough in previous chapters. If, for the moment, you accept the idea that adding complexity is ultimately detrimental and that all security products add complexity, then it is clear that at some point you have to get off the treadmill. At some point, you have to stop installing a new product every time there is a new threat. To do that, you have to find a way (if there is a way) to be future-proof.

In the present world and thus the present market, the opponent enjoys an asymmetric advantage. The opponent has a workfactor that is proportional to the cost of creating a new mechanism of attack. You, the defender, have a workfactor that is proportional to the sum of all methods of attack developed to date, plus the cost of analysis. The opponent can bribe your staff to work against you; you are in no position to offer bribes for continued loyalty (read, "protection"). The opponent has pretty clearly come to have the advantages of automation in crafting new methods, and therefore not only has an asymmetric advantage but also does not have any possibility of labor shortage as a rate-limiting factor for the production of new methods. You, on the other hand, will at most get automation on your side some of the time as truly novel attacks will evade whatever automation you are able to bring to bear and the world's economy has demands for security professionals that clearly outstrip the supply growth of them. (Parenthetically, when the demand for expertise outstrips supply, the fraction of all practitioners that are charlatans tends to rise; be wary.)

This future-proof-ness goal is no joke and no pushover. It is no joke as the rate of attacks of all sorts, inside and outside, as well as the rate at which new tools used to steal data appear, are not just holding up but may be accelerating. (For the purpose of this discussion, we don't care whether an attack tool is a piece of code, a vulnerability in the Internet, or the a new form of social engineering.) Even if the rate of introduction of tools or the attack rate itself were to become constant — only so many new attack mechanisms per quarter — that not mean that you could somehow now ignore the introduction of new threat. Whatever protective gear one has, that gear has a non-zero probability of proving insufficient over time for no other reason than that the problem, and thus the engineering problem statement, mutates.

As an engineer would say, the only way out of such a dilemma is to out-abstract the problem. That is, to find a problem statement that has a well thought generality such that, as new attack tools appear, it can adapt to those new tools. The alternative is that you have to buy and install a new solution every time a new attack tool appears. If you pick that path, "they" win. So the question is whether we know, or know how to find, such an abstraction that we can build solutions which don't time out?

To break this cycle, we have to make compromises. No vendor selling a fabulous solution to a horrid problem will want to hear that they are winning a battle while you are losing a war. A few vendors are different, but most are quite naturally proud of how well they

An example of how things fail: Spam e-mail, which by the way traces back to a husband-and-wife team of Arizona immigration lawyers in 1994, is an obvious example. No matter what you do to stop it, the opposition can adapt and can do so faster than you can react. For every mechanism you put in, they concede the ability of that mechanism to work and simply move on to a new method. Take statistical ("Bayesian") filters: When first introduced they worked marvelously and, which is more, they could be trained; in January, 2005, say, they beat the pants off the opposition. Because a Bayesian filter is statistical, it is all about looking for similarities across sample spaces. The spammers figured that out, and so today, in October, 2007, every spam message is different enough to defeat statistical pattern matching. As you can probably confirm, this same pattern of measure, counter-measure, counter-counter-measure, ... *ad infinitum* goes on in both spam and elsewhere all day every day. That is the cycle we have to find a way to break.

crush whatever it is that they crush, and well they should be. The supply side is giving the demand side what it asked for: known solutions to known problems, with no wasted capabilities. The demand side needs to realize that when it takes all the running you can do to keep in the same place, that you need to rethink why it is you are willing to keep playing the game — just change the rules.

Perhaps the simplest argument is to appeal to an analogy with nature: Which would you rather have, an immune system of your very own, or a paid service that sprays new antibiotics into your air whenever a new pathogen kills somebody?

7.5. Security products as a threat in and of themselves

Security products tend to need and thus to have special powers. As enterprises buy and install them, the special powers the security products have become pervasive, a substrate of function that can be expected to be present wherever you go. Of course, security products are intended for good and always have some degree of self-protection built in. Like a bouncer in a nightclub, they are supposed to be bigger and stronger than the other patrons.

At the same time, a security product that can itself be subverted is an awfully appealing possibility if you are an attacker. If the entity with special powers is on your side, you are better off than if that entity never existed in the first place. The very fact that it has special powers changes the economic equation for you, the attacker, as it makes the return on investment you may receive from co-opting the security tool so much more attractive than what you would receive from brute-forcing your way in. Put differently, why bomb the palace if you can bribe the bodyguard?

There is strong evidence that security products are targeted by the opposition. There is strong suspicion (read, circumstantial evidence) that effective subversion of security tools will not be reported in the press because the subversion will never be made public — it is too valuable to the opposition to brag about it, to flaunt it, or even to prove they have it. Like a mole in an intelligence agency, breaks in security products are too valuable to expose.

The probable existence of breaks in security products changes the equation. As Symantec itself said[47] over a year ago,

> Symantec speculates that while the number of publicly disclosed vulnerabilities could decrease, the window of exposure to potential threats could increase, as details about vulnerabilities are held privately for greater periods of time. This could in turn increase the likelihood of leaked vulnerabilities and the development of privately held exploit code. If vulnerability research becomes increasingly marginalized and moves further underground, enterprises, consumers, and small businesses could face longer windows of exposure, thereby increasing their exposure to potential threats.

While Symantec was talking in general, security products in and of themselves are what really matter here. There is some evidence that the percentage of all attacks that are directed against security products is greater than the percentage that security products are of all products, *i.e.*, security products are over-represented amongst targets. This is, of course, very hard data to get and there is really substantial selection bias in whatever means you use to acquire it, so that leaves us with a traditional tradeoff decision: Is it conservative to assume that a security product will itself be targeted? Yes, of course. Is it conservative to assume that security products need to have special protections built in because they will get special attack pressures? Yes, of course. Is it conservative to assume that the mechanism of successful attacks against security products will be treated as important assets by their misbegotten owners? Yes, of course.

The Witty Worm in 2004 is perhaps the most analyzed. It targeted Internet Security System's BlackICE and RealSecure and it used its invasion of those security products to destroy the computers on which they ran. More recently (2007), the Storm virus has been found to blind anti-virus products to its presence, a presence that is growing.

[47] "Symantec Internet Security Threat Report IX", March, 2006.

As you consider the data security market, one of the half-dozen cardinal virtues you should seek is whether the tool you are considering buying can be re-used as an attack tool. The answer won't be black or white, but some shade of grey. Sherlock Holmes, contemplating a scalpel, said to Watson, "The tools of healing are indistinguishable from the tools of crime." Were he here today, he would probably say the same about the security tools we use. LC5, neé L0PHTcrack, was both a security tool (screening password quality) and an attack tool (and, for a time, was the attack tool of choice). Every system administrator hunting down, say, a rogue DHCP server will employ a tool like Fyodor's `nmap` and/or Hobbit's `ncat`, but, of course, with tools like those intent matters. We could go on and on with this, as you probably well know.

One of the things about security products that makes this all the more important is that for them to run they have to have great powers, hence the first question is whether how easy it is to get inside the security product you are thinking of using. No security vendor takes this lightly, at least for long, and so one of the things you should ask of your security vendor is to see the report of the third-party evaluations of their product that they have already had done. Some of these should be design reviews and some should be penetration tests or, more precisely, what you are looking for is technically a "white-box hostile evaluation." The term of art "white-box" means that the evaluator had access to everything about the product: documentation, training, source code, everything. The term of art "hostile" is what it sounds like, the evaluator should see how far they can get in doing things that were not intended.

Quality assurance sort of does the same thing, but not quite, as QA looks for "Does it do what we wanted it to do?" and that is a job that can be done by lesser mortals. Security assurance looks for "Does it do anything unexpected?" and that is where the outside evaluators are essential as they aren't led by their preconceptions. Figure 33 tries to show this,[48] but, in any case, what you need to insist upon is that such an evaluation

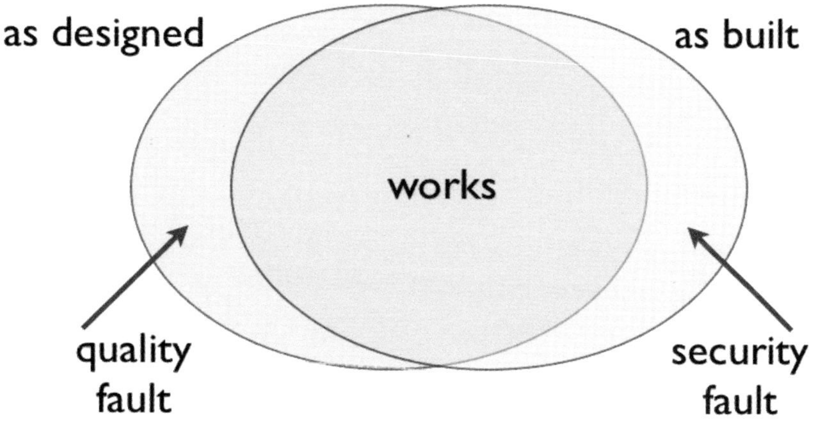

Figure 33: The difference between quality and security

[48] Thompson HH & Whittaker JA, "Testing for Software Security," Dr. Dobbs Journal, v342 p24-34, November, 2002.

has been done and that you get to see it. Note that the mark of a good evaluator is not "We got in!" since, after all, everything is breakable at some price. No, the mark of a good evaluator is "The level of effort to break XYZ is ________." You and your vendor then get to talk about whether you, as the customer, can imagine anyone spending that amount of effort getting at you.

And don't let the vendor say "We wrote it all ourselves!" because that simply does not happen. No one writes complete systems from scratch; they include libraries and modules from all over whether they want to or not. Sometimes they outsource and sometimes their outsourcers outsource again. If that doesn't convince you that a white-box hostile evaluation is a necessity, then events, rather than argument, will be what forces you to revisit the question.

7.6. How to challenge a vendor

When buying a security product, the section headings of this chapter are, in fact, what you need to use to formulate your challenges. If you like having a philosophy, then this by George Santayana should suffice:

> Scepticism is the chastity of the intellect; it is shameful to give it up too soon, or to the first comer.

First, you need to see if you can get your technical and business justifications to match each other and then (only then) see if the vendor's product is a natural fit. It is so very, very common for a security product to assume that you will mold your firm to match the product, when, of course, you want the product to mold itself to match your firm. You'll be better able to do this if you can at first align yourself internally, and then make demands on your vendor. Since most cutting edge security products come from small shops that want to sell to big shops, you'll be able to push them around on this "who conforms to whom" point.

When looking at what to buy, treat the market analysts with the same skepticism that you treat the vendors. Market analysts are, after all, vendors of ideas and (as discussed above) they cannot afford to get to far away from the positions of the vendors themselves. Challenge your vendors, both for the product and for the market analysis, to justify why this, of all the options, is actually not just the new color for handbags this fall but is instead something that is lasting. The whole thing about future-proofness is that idea, and you need to let the counterparty say "Look how cool this is!" about twenty times before you say "But how will it be next season?" Nothing takes the steam out of a point solution like generality over time or space, and nothing takes the steam out of a purported general solution like an examination of whether its complexity leads to instability. Remember, your cost of integration and operation will exceed the cost of license.

And complexity is a real challenge. What vendors claim and what they deliver have to sum to ever more complexity in their products. This can mean that there is no way you'll ever use all the features that are present, and it can mean that things that sound too good to be true generally are. Some marks for a product being complex are to see whether it must be installed by them, not you, whether upgrades are irreversible or can be backed out, and/or whether integrating the security product with the rest of your environment is a one-of-a-kind effort requiring the vendor's own staff. Another is whether when problems do occur that the vendor has to send a chief engineer to you, or whether patch releases are frequent enough to be a measurable operational load on you. Yet another mark of complexity is where the number of configuration parameters is such that it unlikely that anyone has or could test all possible combinations of them. And yet another is where there are six different ways to do anything — which is not bad, *per se*, but guarantees that it will often be difficult to recover the "Why are we doing this?" from the "Here is what the config file says we are doing."

The hard question of whether the solution you are considering is itself future-proof can sometimes be addressed. To demonstrate the point, consider a tool that offers some protection against so-called zero-day (0day) attacks, attacks which use a previously unknown method and therefore cannot already have a direct counter to them installed. To model this, take whatever platform you like, Windows XP, say, and install a machine with the original distribution of that product, *i.e.*, with no patches but only the original installation media. Now, install your tool that, it is hoped, protects against 0days. Finally, take all the attacks[49] that have been detected since the original release of (in this case) Windows XP and fire them at the unpatched machine that is running your protective software.

If your software does succeed in protecting the operating system against such a flood of attacks, you can declare a particular kind of victory. No, you cannot truly predict the future but, in this case, you took all the future that Windows XP had in front of it from the day of release to whatever day you run your test, and used that to confirm that had your product been available when XP was released that the 0days since then would not have mattered. This is a mechanism of test that is unique to the digital world as only in the digital world can the past be recreated with fidelity and the future played on fast forward. Of course, past performance is not a guarantee of future results, but you can simulate the future by replaying the past if you are careful about how you do it, careful in the sense of not misleading yourself or others.

Security products can be, and should be regarded as, a threat in and of themselves. Never mistake obscurity of mechanism for true security unless you are willing to bet your farm on never having an insider attack. Here's the though experiment: Take your most trusted insider, humiliate them in public, offend their honor, and throw them out on the street daring them to do their worst. If once on the street they are no more threat

---

[49] One place to look for such a repository of malware is `www.wildlist.org/`

than the panhandler at the corner, then you have a security regime that does not rely on obscurity. If not, then you don't. When you buy a security product, you are betting that none of your vendor's staff could hurt you if, somehow, you became their target in an adrenaline-fueled moment.

Remember, the first measure of success for an external attacker is gaining the access, authority, and trust afforded to an insider, nearly no one has a crisp line between inside and outside, and therefore the threat you must model is that of a digital insider. Put differently, the reason to have a security regime that is proof against the insider is that it tends to solve the external attack as a side effect.

7.7. The next wave

But, seriously, where does all the bad news from the data security front lead? If we think of this as a kind of evolution, then we might want to remember what we know of the biological world. First, predators are the reason prey evolve and diversify. We are prey, the predator pressure is real, and if we don't evolve and diversify[50] we won't make it. Second, that if a mechanism of attack is wildly virulent the reason is almost surely that the protection (immune) system is pretty

[50] Geer D, Bace R, Gutmann P, Metzger P, Pfleeger C, Quarterman JS & Schneier B, "Cyberinsecurity: The Cost of Monopoly," Computer & Communications Industry Association, Washington, D.C., 23 September 2003 www.ccianet.org/papers/cyberinsecurity.pdf

good at stopping (killing) it thus the need to move quickly; only those things which evade immune systems can afford to go slowly (which is why wide epidemics of computer viruses become ever rarer per unit interval but become ever faster moving when they do strike). Third, that infectious agents rarely cross species boundaries so a little diversity goes a long way if you are in a situation where security is a subset of reliability. Fourth, that corruption of the immune system itself is the worst (*cf.*, HIV in people to Witty in firewalls). Fifth, that parasites do not want to kill their hosts but rather co-exist with them non-lethally, which is why some believe that hosts in botnets may be better managed after infection than they were before. Sixth, and as said before, change and trouble don't come evenly spaced, they come in bunches.

To go forward, "we" — all of us — need a new model for data protection. Since we've already said it once, let's say it again, in engineering, including security engineering, it is the problem statement that limits what is produced. Those problem statements, like the security products they imagine, profit from simplicity. With that said, here are the minimalist Requirements (it is not a solution unless present), the Constraints (it is not a solution if present), and the Desirables (it is a better solution when present) for a data security product that might stand the test of time and hostile evaluation both.

R1	Protect all data
R2	Make that protection adjustable
R3	Know the protection status of all data at all times
C1	Do not rely on the sentience of human operators
C2	Do not rely on the cooperation of human operators
C3	Recovery has no role, only protection
D1	Have value-creating side effects
D2	Be very nearly future-proof
D3	Low/no cost to good people doing good things

Those are, of course, harder than they look and each of them may create a number of sub-requirements, but the core idea is that everything can be valuable, that run-time modifications are valuable if limited, and that becoming confused over whether the protections are working or not negates the value of those protections. At the same time, if you believe that your threat model has to be that of a digital insider (whether directly true or because an outsider is already on the inside), then data protection has to be applied with the data, not with the network nor with the central processing unit (CPU). Finally, if the security regime can enable other things yours is a happy world indeed, if the product is future proof it is already a long way towards being cost effective, and to get in the way of good people is always a crime whenever it isn't necessary.

That all says something simple, actually: Going forward data is our focus. Data security is what distinguishes data which has value from data which does not. A rising threat requires any defensive perimeter to contract, and that statement is true for the military, it is true for wildebeeste, and it is true for data. A contracted perimeter for data shifts the unit of protection from networks and servers to individual data objects at their point of use.

Why? Because data is at risk when and where it changes from at-rest to in-motion, you should think of that as state-change (like evaporation). That point-of-use, where that state change occurs, becomes the locus of your data security efforts. Monitoring is the first priority since you cannot control what you cannot see, or, as U.S. Sec. of Defense Donald Rumsfeld famously said, it's the unknown unknowns that will kill you.

There have been some stabs at this, but they haven't done much in reality.

- Content inspection tries to examine network transmissions on the wire and in real time, but that means the only person you catch is the one who doesn't know or doesn't care that you are watching since content inspection can be defeated by Pig Latin, much less encryption. (Content inspection by scanning all your files *in situ* can certainly be valuable in same way a tourniquet can be valuable — it stops a hemorrhage you can't yet suture or, in the case of data, it stops inadvertent data hemorrhages you haven't yet sutured with thoroughgoing data classification.)
- Statistical anomaly detection tries to highlight the odd and assumes a human takes it from there.

Basically, this trades off an infeasible work factor to damp out false positives with the risk factor of what events that would have been valuable to detect are missed.

- Signature finding, the way anti-virus, anti-malware, anti-spyware, and so forth do is just an insurmountable work factor for you and will always trail the need.

Summing up the future, attacks where the attacker does not have to show himself must be preempted, but preemption requires intelligence, and intelligence requires surveillance. Therefore, and this is a serious fork in the road, you have to pick a surveillance structure which means you have to pick a unit of observation. There are only two obvious ones: you either surveil a known person and watch what they do with data not previously identified, or you surveil known data and watch who does what with that data. If surveillance is total, they are equivalent, but in any case the records of the latter — surveilling data — are safer to have around and are directly aligned with watching what is valuable in proportion to its value. Repeating for emphasis,

Attacks where the attacker does not have to show himself must be preempted,
but preemption requires intelligence, and intelligence requires surveillance.

8. What we have learned

Continual progress is fanning out the kinds of places data lives and the number of ways it goes, and so data security will have to be built in rather than bolted on. This may well require relying on hardware support, a topic of vibrant research outside the scope of this book, and it may also require making data security a principal focus of the enterprise with both a surveillance and an interdiction component.

I am convinced that the time for half-measures is, for better or worse, behind us and that only an invisible and inescapable security regime, one that does not get in the way of getting the work of the enterprise done, will do. One might argue that meeting such a challenge is still premature, but one cannot argue that meeting such a challenge is not inevitable.

We are kidding ourselves if we think that the attractive benefits of the digital lifestyle, whether for persons or companies, don't come with a serious price in the form of data control. As bits replace atoms as the chief constituent of modern life, what those bits represent, *viz.*, data, becomes what we have, what we have to control, and how it is that we achieve that control. While Stewart Brand was the first to say "Information wants to be free," to repeat only that is to miss his point, which he restated in print[51] in this way:

Information wants to be free.
Information wants to be expensive.
That tension will not go away.

This book is based on the premise that information wants to be expensive and free, with the fine line controlled by the owner of that information. That may not be fair, but neither is life. Such conclusions are neither pleasant nor fashionable, but they are nonetheless true: The price of an interconnected, interdependent, always-on digital world is data control.

[51] The Media Lab: Inventing the Future at MIT, MIT Press, 1987, p202.